Thurrock's Past: Echoes from a Place

Lejins Publishing

First Published in 1997

by

Lejins Publishing
Stanford-le-Hope
Essex SS17 0HY

ISBN   0 9528789 0 9

In partnership with
Thurrock Museum,
a service provided by Thurrock Council

British Library Cataloguing in Publication Data
is available for this book

Printed and bound in Great Britain by
Redwood Books, Trowbridge, Wiltshire

ACKNOWLEDGEMENTS

Thanks to John Webb, Thurrock Local History Society; Alan Gosling, Purfleet Heritage and Military Centre; Vic Tucker, Grays Library; Terry Carney and Jonathan Catton, Thurrock Museum; Thurrock CVS.

A special thanks to Randal Bingley, who provided the inspiration and encouragement.

And finally, thanks to all those authors whose works have been included in this volume; most of whom now exist only through their writings and through the memory of others.

Cover illustration: detail from a sketch of a view by St Clement's Church, West Thurrock by Miss Katherine Fry (1870)

FOREWORD

Next to *human* love, no affection seems so strong as that which most of us feel for *place.* We all have a *somewhere* which speaks out in its personal way, making us feel at home; at ease.

Since life happens to have cast me an exile from my own especial part of the home-counties, I know just how bitter-sweet it can be to have some remembered landscape-image brought to mind; perhaps triggered by a picture, a phrase of music, or even (for me) by the scent of damp bracken-roots among Langdon Hill's woods. Any of these kinds of things may give the required identity-fix, helping us to see again more sharply what it is we think we are.

That is why I like so much Alan Leyin's attractively-schemed anthology about *this* place - this nook of Essex hemmed in by a winding Thames and backed by those always-changing northward hills which provide nowadays each morning my pleasant kitchen view.

One has to pan the murky stream of printer's ink a long, long while for any gold-bearing mineral to gleam through, so I can guess what this fascinating anthology represents in downright application. It is full of the flavours of our district and its people, as seen across the centuries by various (generally passerine) authors and it contains not a few of those scintillating nuggets of local literature which we've maybe stumbled upon in library books, or midst the leaves of old magazines, but could never quite manage to find again.

Some sunny day, I'll take *my* copy of this charming collection to the fern-deep top of Langdon Hills, overlooking Thurrock's *prodigious valley,* and read it clean through; enjoying a breath of both my life's places at once.

Randal Bingley

INTRODUCTION

Of the Thameside villages in the eastern part of Thurrock, the following was written *"But these... hamlets are all doomed in time to disappear, and the smiling villages of a once radiant riverside will finally be buried in a concretion of suburban villas, brick terraces, and teeming factories. Let us note and admire them while we may; for ere long they will have vanished, and be lost beyond all possible recovery."* These words, now *themselves* echoes, almost lost in time, were written in 1902. [1]

At the current time, when the local landscape is undergoing a period of such unprecedented development, many people would share the above concerns. Obviously change cannot be stemmed. However, it can be managed: responsibly, or just indifferently. Reference to the past is the only measure we have of the quality of progress.

There are now a number of local publications, mainly pictorial, that enable us to record these changes. Pictorial records are useful, and justifiably popular. However, whilst they undoubtedly show what the local area *was* like, they do not always convey feelings and experiences of those people who lived at the time. This collection of writings is meant to go some way to redress the balance: to show the delight, the distress, the enthusiasms of those who have gone before.

Whilst things inevitably change; some things remain constant. The Thames, as one of the world's most important waterways, has always been a significant feature of Thurrock: shaping both the landscape and the people. Its mark is well documented by the number of references in this anthology. With the more recent development of road and rail networks, the significance of the river may now no longer be as apparent as it once was - but the Thames still ebbs and flows quietly through the landscape: now, as it did then... ever changing, but ever constant. This link between the Thames and Thurrock, and indeed with all nations, is clear and is captured on the motto of Thurrock's Coat of Arms: *"By Thames to all peoples of the world".*

---

[1] Clark, P. *Vanishing Essex Villages: an Undiscovered Corner.* 1902.

THE VIEWS FROM THE HIGH LANDS...

Writers and travellers, of ages past, when describing Thurrock's landscape, often captured the once picturesque and panoramic local views, with the Thames appearing as a prominent feature. Of the land around Grays, the Revd. William Palin, Rector of Stifford, in 1871, wrote:

"The views from the high lands of Grays are extensive and beautiful, embracing the whole river Thames from Purfleet to the Lower Hope, beyond Gravesend, with its ever-moving panorama of ships hoisting the flag of every civilised nation of the earth, pleasantly varied by the merry little river steamers, waking up sleepy people by their well-meaning brass bands. Considering the singular beauty of the prospect, and the exceptionally healthy soil, gravel and chalk throughout, and South aspect, its not being sought more widely for building can only be from its advantages being unknown except to those who are enjoying them."

Rev. William J.T. Palin, 1871.
Stifford and its Neighbourhood: Past and Present.

1

BOLDLY RISING HILLS...

Of the land which extends from Little Thurrock, east to Fobbing, a 19th century Directory is equally enthusiastic, recording a rural landscape of some beauty. But still the Thames is featured.

"... (The land) extends about 14 miles along the north bank of the River Thames, from Gravesend Reach and Tilbury Fort to Canvey Island... it is a fertile and picturesque district with many handsome seats, neat villages, and boldly rising hills, commanding extensive views of the Thames down to the ocean."

William White, 1863.
History, Gazetteer and Directory of the County of Essex.

"Boldly rising hills" may not be features that first come to mind when describing the current landscape around the Thames. The dramatic effect obtained from the *"high lands"* is now often obscured by the residential and industrial developments along the low lying banks of the river. However, with a little local knowledge there are places where these views can be appreciated: where all vessels of the world can still be observed moving quietly along the great waterway into the mighty oceans and on to distant lands.

AND VANISH INTO LIGHT...

Further inland few would argue that the hills do indeed rise *"boldly".* Areas where extensive views can be readily found and appreciated; again with the ever changing backdrop of the Thames. For some travellers the effect of the ever-changing prospect of the river was such that it moved them to poetry.

"The stately river was dotted with ships outward and inward bound, from the mighty ocean steamer (so dwarfed by distance that it was difficult to realise that the tiny moving speck with the long trail of smoke behind was actually a little world afloat) to the humble barge; several of these picturesque craft were noticeable on the water, their many sails, light in the sunshine and dark in the shade, added greatly to the effect of the picture by the life they gave to it, and as they glided downward with the tide we watched them...

*pass on and on, and go
From less to less, and vanish into light'..."*

*James Hissey, 1889.
In P. Lindley, (ed.) New Holidays in Essex.*

THE FINEST PROSPECTS IN ENGLAND...

By 1863 the *"high lands"* of Thurrock were becoming quite popular with tourists, particularly with visiting *"pleasure parties from the metropolis"*.

"LAINDON HILLS... The hill on which the parish stands is about a mile in length and breath, and its summit commands one of the finest prospects in England extending over the vale of the Thames from London to the Nore...

Pleasure parties from the metropolis and other places often assemble around a large tree on the highest point, to enjoy the extensive and delightful view, in which is seen the broad bosom of the Thames for a distance of nearly 40 miles, thickly studded with steam and sailing vessels; and a wide range of country in this county and Kent."

William White, 1863.
History, Gazetteer and Directory of the County of Essex.

4

ON THIS HER HIGH ALTAR...

The *"large tree at the highest point"* referred to in the last section must have been a well known vantage point. Another encounter with it, and with a *"picnic party"*, is recorded here.

> *"Ascending the summit, we stand in the parish of LAINDON HILLS, and there lies unrolled before us one of the most beautiful views in the county, aye, in the kingdom, for it was not long ago observed 'Essex may justly boast here of the grandest prospect in England.' The rich vale of the Thames, to which the step hill-side falls abruptly - the river with its shipping - the grim battlements at Tilbury, with the signs of the signs of the city which they guard seen dimly beyond - and the opposite coast of Kent traceable up to the Medway, form altogether a scene worthy of the pilgrimage of the picnic party whom we found seated beneath the tree which stands on the topmost crown of the hill, enjoying the prospect, and worshipping Nature on this her high altar."*

D.W. Coller, 1861.
The Peoples' History of Essex.

THE MOST ASTONISHING PROSPECTS...

Earlier travellers also held the local views in high regard. Perhaps, in the following piece, we should allow for some poetic license... but certainly the high ground on the Bagshot Sands of Langdon Hills was, and still is, an area of beauty and dramatic effect. At these earlier times, the areas seemed to have escaped the *"picnic parties"*.

"... near Horndon, on the summit of a vast hill, one of the most astonishing prospects to be beheld, breaks almost at once upon one of the dark lanes. Such a prodigious valley, every where painted with the finest verdure, and intersected with numberless hedges and woods, appears beneath you, that it is past description; the Thames winding thro' it, full of ships, and bounded by the hills of Kent. Nothing can exceed it, unless that which Hannibal exhibited to his disconsolate troops, when he bade them behold the glories of the Italian plains! If ever a turnpike should lead through this country, I beg you will go and view this enchanting scene, though a journey of 40 miles is necessary for it. I never beheld anything equal to it in the West of England, that, region of landscape."

Arthur Young, 1767.
King's Head, (West) Tilbury.
A Six Weeks' Tour Through the Southern Counties of England and Wales. 1772.

INDULGED WITH A FULL ENJOYMENT...

The following description records that, in 1808, the visitors travelled to Langdon Hills from Tilbury; indicating that they travelled to Tilbury via the Thames. This illustrates the importance of the Thames as a means of travel until the London-Tilbury railway was established in 1854.

"A carriage was provided for us at Tilbury, and in the course of two hours reached the summit of Langdon Hill. Here I was gratified with the most delightful prospects my eyes ever beheld. Lady Tracy (of Billericay) caused the carriage to stop at certain intervals, that her daughter and I might be indulged with a full enjoyment of it; while she, to whom it was familiar, pointed out to us the most material objects. The country before us formed a beautiful enclosed valley, bounded towards the west and south-west by the distant hills of Highgate and Hampstead, and the Surrey hills, within which wide circuit appeared the great emporium of Europe, the city of London; thence I could trace the beautiful meanderings of the Thames, and the quantities of shipping passing and repassing. I saw the village of Tilbury below, Gravesend, with the chalk cliffs of Kent and the country rising like a vast amphitheatre from the marshes. Turning towards the east we discovered the conjunction of the Thames with the Medway, and the view was terminated by the blue tints of the salt sea, where it opens into the mouth of the British Channel."

Joseph Strutt, 1808.
Queenhoo Hall.
(In) An Anthology of Essex.

Joseph Strutt died before this novel was finished. However, it was published with the final two chapters written by Sir Walter Scott. The success of the novel inspired Scott to complete his own great works.

FILLS THE MIND WITH QUIET PLEASURE...

S ome travellers shunned the carriage in favour of a walk to the "summit" to discover the *"pretty nooks and secluded hollows"*.

"A few miles farther and we stop at Stanford-le-Hope, a village pleasantly situated on an eminence not far from that broadening reach of the river known as The Hope. It has a church worth looking at, standing on the brow, amid an environment of corn-fields, whence you get a good view of Horndon-on-the-Hill.

I made haste to walk thither, wishful to mount yet higher before sunset. About half an hour sufficed. I left my knapsack at the Bell, and started afresh for an hour's walk on the road to Billericay, which presently begins to rise, and becoming lane-like, with high hedges and honeysuckle blooms on each side, mounts to the top of the Langdon hills. I got over a gate, and rambled about knee-deep in fern, among the ash, oaks, and elms that adorn the summit, seeking the best points of view.

The height is not great - three hundred and eighty eight feet - but the prospect is vast: one that occupies the eye and fills the mind with quiet pleasure. Forty miles of the Thames and its estuary lie before you; Shooter's Hill appears as a rounded mass in the distance; the Crystal Palace and St Paul's can be seen in favourable states of the atmosphere; and when night comes on the dwellers on and around the Langdons see the glow of London in the distant sky. Eastwards, broad levels, brightened here and there by the gleam of a creek, contrast with the great undulating slope that rushes down to meet them. Westwards there stretches away to a pale blue distance, over a region thickly bestrewn with villages, and apparently endless succession of farms and fields, alternate patches of green and yellow, and over all the landscape the warmth and softness prevail that belong to wood; and this wood closes the north-western horizon with forest-like masses. Trees grow thickly on the flanks of the hills themselves, and in places you look between the stems as through a long glade, down upon the scene beneath. You may wander about at will, discovering pretty nooks and secluded hollows and open knolls; and on the left of the road a cool clear spring close by a copse where the ground is half hidden by ferns, and the sky by the graceful foliage of the birch.

For me there was an additional charm - that of sunset; and I sauntered, now in a broad stream of the golden light, now in some hollows where it flickered through the maze of branches; and when I came forth to retrace my steps, the sky looked glorious with its array of ruddy clouds."

Walter White, 1865.
Eastern England from the Thames to the Humber.

The reference to Crystal Palace, may need some explanation: in 1852, Crystal Palace was relocated from Hyde Park to Sydenham. So that most spectacular landmark, at the time the above was written, was south of the river.

ALL THIS GOODLY PROSPECT...

Having noted the enthusiasms of previous travellers, no section on Langdon hills would be complete without more exuberant words from James Hissey, who seems to capture, in no uncompromising terms, the beauty of the landscape.

"It is astonishing that a spot of so much beauty (possessing a peculiar character all of its own, and not to be repeated in England) should be so near to town and so little known... From where we stood we looked down through the sun-filled air upon a glorious expanse of waving woods, green meadows and red tilled fields, down upon miles of smiling verdure, dotted here and there with scattered farmsteads, red-roofed villages, and ever and again a peep of a distant church tower or spire. All this goodly prospect, bounded only be the circling blue of the far away horizon, where land and sky were blended together in a dim, dreamy uncertainty. Right through the heart of this map-like panorama wound the silvery Thames, or so it seemed to us... our vision rejoiced in its unaccustomed freedom, confined as it is for so great a portion of the year to the sadly limited vista of a London Street...

This of English views is certainly unique in one respect, the prospect - which, by the way, comes suddenly upon the observer and gains greatly by the fact - is uninterrupted in all direction, and the Thames, widening to a mighty river here, gives a sense of vastness to the scene more suggestive of Western America, that land of big rivers, mighty distances and broad effects."

James Hissey, 1889.
In P. Lindley, (ed.) New Holidays in Essex.

The last paragraph may seem to be, perhaps, a little too enthusiastic. Pusey (1987), makes the same point noting that the writer *"... ends with a touch of near-ludicrous hyperbole"*. We can be sure that such comment would not have deterred Mr Hissey from his enthusiasm.

A TOWN OF SOME PRETENSION...

Down on Thurrock's shoreline the scenes were, at one time, equally engaging... but not always as enchanting. The new commercial activities of one wharf certainly did little to enhance the local prospect.

> *"Grays Thurrock... partakes of a picturesque and commercial character, and is a town of some pretension. It stands at the mouth of a creek, and had a pier 400 feet long, at which many passenger steamers plying upon the Thames called, and a regular communication was kept up with the opposite shore. The pier was built by a company in 1841... but the rivalry of the railway has drawn off its traffic, and it is degraded to the purpose of a dung-wharf."*
>
> *D.W. Coller, 1861.*
> *The Peoples' History of Essex.*

A PLEASANT LOOKING PLACE...

Not all towns suffered such indignity from the introduction of commerce and industry. Purfleet, with its cliffs standing proudly against the river, managed, for a while, to form a harmony between beauty and industry - with visitors to the old chalk quarries being a testimony to this.

"A few minutes more and we have crossed West Thurrock marshes and arrived at Purfleet; a place well worth a visit, as we shall see on alighting. It occupies the only high ground on the Essex side between London and Gravesend, and is remembered by steamboat passengers as a pleasant-looking place, nor does it disappoint expectation on a nearer view. To me, and doubtless to others, its special charm is that it is not overbuilt or cockneyfied. 'It belongs,' as the gatekeeper at the Botany will tell you, 'to Government and Mr Whitbread, and neither of 'em allows any houses to be built.' Long may their prohibition continue; for a pleasanter spot than Purfleet for a half-holiday is hardly to be found within the same distance of London. One of the great rounded hills composed of chalk, gravel and clay which prevail with such pleasing effect in other parts of Essex, here advances boldly upon the Thames, and having been largely excavated in past years, now greets the visitor with touches of the romantic and picturesque among its quiet features.

Honeysuckle and pretty flower-gardens beautify the village, as we see while walking through to the western height, where a long high pitched wall, marked 'W.D.' encloses the Royal Powder Magazine, a great tall tank, and other properties of the War Department. Following this wall we come to a brow which on the right terminates in a high bold cliff, whence we can look down on such fruitful well-sheltered gardens in the hollow beneath, on such cosy meadows, with the little chapel standing among them, and on peaks and bluffs of chalk and pinnacles of clay, as will at once inspire us with a most pleasing impression of Purfleet. And by gaps here and there in the hedge we can pass to the jutting points of the cliff, and survey the scene with advantage, and on Sundays hear faintly the simple music of the psalm sung by the village congregation in the chapel below."

Walter White, 1865.
Eastern England from the Thames to the Humber.

YET ANOTHER HEIGHT TO VISIT...

The reference, in the previous passage, to Mr Whitbread, is indeed to the family whose name is associated with the brewing industry. In 1791 Samuel Whitbread built his residence in Purfleet: Purfleet House. To this day, on certain older properties in Purfleet, one can see inscribed the initials "S.W.", clearly identifying them as part of the Whitbread estate.

"This is yet another height to visit. We call at a house near the hotel for a 'ticket for Botany,' and retrace our way through the village to a gate in the wooded bank which stretches riverwards from the railway-station. A man who passed seeing me try to open the gate said, "If you want to go in you must holler Sansum." So I called "Sansum," and was presently admitted by an ancient man, who came from somewhere among the foliage, and led me forthwith to an alcove screened by trees, and pointing to the 'W' in the smooth pebbles of the floor, said, "That stands for Whitbread; and the other two, 'H.P.', are for Henry Palk, who was the librarian to the House of Commons." I remarked that it was very kind of Mr Whitbread to admit the public to such an agreeable place, and the ancient man replied, "Yes, it is kind. There's nothing to pay, only Mr Whitbread don't object to a small present to the gatekeeper, as a sort of acknowledgement, you know, for the free admission." It was impossible to withhold a sixpence from such a simple-minded way of stating the case. Besides, once past the alcove, you may wander at will.

This, in the local phrase, is 'the Bot'ny': the height, for the most part thickly wooded is Beacon Hill. You may ascend to the top by gradual slopes along the front, or by sharp steep zigzags on the flank, where the chalk has been hewn away, leaving cliffs nearly a hundred feet high, and in some places detached masses, now stained and weather-worn. The extent of the excavation shows how large has been the demand for chalk for ballast, and to get out flints for the gun-flint factory once established here. The lower recesses, overspread with soft grass, are delightful playgrounds, shaded here and there by small plantations, and backed by a fruitful orchard. The slopes bear oak, fir, ash and hazel, and a thick under-growth with all the tangle in which Nature delights; so that you may find walks to suit your mood, from the quiet gloom of the rearward slope, with peeps into the fields, to the open paths of the front. On the summit stands a small lighthouse, built by the Admiralty, some years ago, for experimental purposes, whence the prospect is striking and animated."

Walter White, 1865.
Eastern England from the Thames to the Humber.

A TONGUE OF LAND...

The Thames features prominently in all the previous descriptions. As well as adding unquestioned attraction to the locality, the Thames also had a more significant role in shaping the local landscape: one which affected the very shape of the local parishes. Thurrock's early administrative systems were shaped by the flow of the Thames.

"Of the way in which the Thames was a necessary great road in early times, perhaps the best proof is the manner in which various parishes manage to get their water front at the expense of a somewhat unnatural shape to their boundaries... curious and interesting arrangements of this sort of thrusting down from the hills a tongue of land which ends in a wharfage on the river..."

Hilaire Belloc, 1914.
The Historic Thames.

Although Belloc used a parish upriver as an example of this *"tongue of land"*, he could have used any one of Thurrock's waterfront parishes to illustrate his point - with Stifford being a particularly good example. The salt marsh around the banks of the Thames was particularly good grazing ground; another reason why the area was sought after. The inland parishes, not having access to the Thames, were able to use the fens for purposes of grazing their livestock.

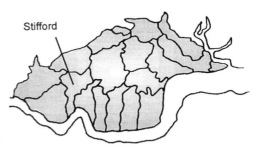

Thurrock's Parishes

BUT MANY LINGERED...

The Thames was not the only influence on the local administrative systems: within its broad reach, and the tranquillity of the local landscape, the inhabitants were attempting to assert their own influence... with whispers of sinister plots. Whilst the following passage is from a novel, the theme is well rooted in Thurrock's past.

"It was a bright Sunday evening in the spring of the year of grace 1381. The Essex bank of the Thames shone like an emerald. The fair church of Fobbing, which crowned the slope, had just poured out its worshippers after Vespers, and dismissed them to their homes; but many lingered behind, and were to be seen hanging about near the churchyard after the service was over, and talking earnestly one to another.

Nothing could be sweeter and more peaceful than the expanse of the Thames, as he displayed his broad smiling face between the slope and shell-haven... Kent bounded the prospect beyond, and the evening sun gilded the vast woods which covered the high ground which separates the Thames from the Medway.

The countenances of the group were not in harmony, however, with the peaceful scene which invited their thankfulness. Scowling looks and a dogged and sullen expression were observable in those who were listeners; whilst a fierce, scornful manner and glance distinguished one who seemed to be a kind of leader amongst them, and who was listened to with the greatest attention.

Rev. W. E. Heygate, 1860.
Alice of Fobbing: or the Times of Jack Straw and Wat Tyler.

Thus was the beginnings of the Peasants' Revolt: a bloody uprising, in 1381.

WHAT SAY YOU, MEN OF FOBBING?

The rebellion was against the increasing poll-taxes, and against the unscrupulous activities of the tax collectors.

"I say it is a shame that we are to pay poll-tax, and have neither glory nor safety. Let us pay for ourselves, and fight for others. Not another groat will they have here. What say you men of Fobbing? What say you?"

"We have paid one, and we pay not again," was the answer.

Rev. W. E. Heygate, 1860.
Alice of Fobbing: or the Times of Jack Straw and Wat Tyler.

It is here where we can let actual history take over. Grieve (1982) records *"The Fobbing villagers' spokesperson, Thomas Baker, who was their collector, who protested that Fobbing had already paid its poll-tax, and brandished the receipt to prove it."*

And so the rebellion started, with the villagers of Fobbing, Corringham and Stanford-le-Hope being the first to show their discontent by marching on the King's judiciary at Brentwood.

Of the 145 rebels named as ringleaders of the Essex rising, no fewer than 28 came from Fobbing which Grieve (1982) records as *"... an astonishing number for a tiny village at the world's end out on the marshes."*

WITH THE MEN OF HIS VILLAGE...

From this small beginning, in the marshlands of the Thames estuary, the uprising rapidly spread to other parts of the country:

> *"[Because of the burdens imposed by these taxes, the local peasants] ...refused to bear such injuries any longer. They conferred together as to what remedial action or assistance could be found. And after each man had pondered on these problems... a certain Thomas Baker of Fobbing took courage and began to exhort and ally himself with the men of his village. These men leagued themselves with others and in turn they contacted their friends and relations so that their message passed from village to village and area to area."*

> *Henry Knighton.*
> *Chronicon. (Ed.) J.R. Lumby, 1889-95.*

Whilst the rebellion gained force, it was ultimately unsuccessful. Thomas Baker of Fobbing was drawn and hanged at Chelmsford in July 1381.

Eight other men of Fobbing also paid dearly for their part in the uprising:

William Gildeborn	Hanged
Thomas Gildeborn	A fugitive
Richard Frannceys	Hanged; his goods seized
John Wolk	Hanged; his goods seized
John Delvin	His goods seized
Ralph White	His goods seized
Richard Tripat	A fugitive
Robert Knight	A fugitive; his goods seized, among them a boat with all its gear.

THE AGUE AND ITS EVILS...

Not all hazards were a consequence of "ill deeds": other hazards were more natural. The "Ague", as it was known, was a sickness which was little understood at the time.

"I have read with interest an article on vanishing Essex villages... The writer, Percy Clarke, BA., has entirely omitted... any mention of the ague very general in the parishes of Fobbing, Corringham, Mucking, Tilbury and adjoining districts. I speak from personal knowledge. About forty seven years ago (1854) I was curate of the parish of Laindon, and was well acquainted with the beneficed clergy and their curates of the above-mentioned parishes, and I can testify, that after a year's residence, ague was the cause of more than one of them resigning their livings, particularly in Fobbing and Corringham. Of course the building of sea walls, and superior systems of drainage of the marshy lands and inland creeks of mud and salt water on the Essex side of the river Thames, may in some favoured localities, have partly modified the fever of which I complain. But I have a lively remembrance of the ague and its evils, for I, more than once I believe, had narrowly escaped from its constantly recurring and weakening effects even on the strongest constitutions. The usually remedy prescribed by our medical advisers was frequent doses of Quinine or Jesuits Bark and, when obtainable, some forty year old Port wine. But one cure suggested was to swallow a tablespoonful of gunpowder, and immediately after to take violent exercise, i.e. run a few miles and so get into a complete perspiration. One person to whom I related the gunpowder cure, rather ridiculed it, and suggested that undoubtedly the most complete remedy for the ague, would be to fill one's mouth with gunpowder and then set a lighted match to it! It was customary in my Essex days, to

avoid going out of doors after sunset, for an hour or so; and windows used to be closed about that period of the evening, to keep out the aguish miasma as it arose after sun-down from the undrained marshy creeks and lands surrounding the parish of Fobbing and its contiguous villages."

Wm. Gibbens, 1902.
The Essex Review.

The parishes referred to above were, at the time, known as "Kill priest", as so many curates fell to the *"aguish miasma"*. John Pell - Rector of Fobbing and Laindon from 1661 to 1685 - however, did not fall to the ague. But in those days it was not unusual for Rectors to live outside their parishes; indeed Pell did spend much time outside his parish. Nevertheless, he was still sufficiently troubled by the prospect of the ague to make his concerns known. When Pell complained to the Archbishop of Canterbury about the unhealthyness of his parish, he was reassured, *"I doe not intend that you shall live there."* To which Pell replied, *"No, but your Grace does intend that I shall die there."*

Had Pell suffered a similar fate to that of many of his curates, mathematics, as we know it today, would have been very different. Pell was a mathematician of some International acclaim, and is noted for inventing the division sign.

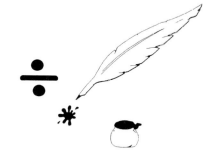

Although he escaped the ague, it is recorded that Pell *"dyed of a broaken heart."*

AMONG THE FOGS AND DAMPS...

The ague had obviously been around these marshes for many years. In his travels through Thurrock, Daniel Defoe, author of *Robinson Crusoe*, made reference to it in 1724.

"I have one remark more, before I leave this damp part of the world, and which I cannot omit on the woman's account; namely, that I took notice of a strange decay of the sex here; insomuch, that all along this county it was very frequent to meet men that had had from five to six, to fourteen or fifteen wives; nay, and some more; and I was informed that in the marshes on the other side the river over-against Candy (Canvey) Island, there was a farmer, who was then living with the five and twentieth wife, and that his son who was about 35 years old, had already had about fourteen; indeed this part of the story, I only had by report, though from good hands to, about Fobbing, Curringham, Thundersly... and other towns of the like situation... The reason, as a merry fellow told me, who said he had had about a dozen and half of wives, (though I found afterwards he fibbed a little) was this; that they being bred in the marshes themselves, and seasoned to the place, did pretty well with it; but that they always went up into the hilly country, or to speak their own language into the uplands for a wife: that when they took the young lasses out of the wholesome and fresh air, they were healthy, fresh and clear, and well; but when they came out of their native air into the marshes among the fogs and damps, there they presently changed their complexion, got an ague or two, and seldom held it above half a year, or a year at most; and then, said he, we go to the uplands again, and fetch another; so that marrying of wives was reckoned a kind of good farm to them. It is true, the fellow told this in a kind of drollery, and mirth; but the fact, for all of that, is certainly true; and that they have an abundance of wives by that very means."

Daniel Defoe, 1724.
A Tour Through the Whole Island of Great Britain.

THE SCENT OF GRASS AND HEDGEROWS

Although Defoe implies that *"the uplands"* were immune from the reaches of the ague, this was by no means always the case.

> *"On my return to The Bell I had a talk with Mrs Spurgeon, the hostess, while she folded the heap of newly-dried household linen that filled the room with. One of her topics was her family connections with the famous preacher; another, the recent occurrence of cases of ague in Horndon. The like had not been known for years. It was natural enough to expect ague at Pitsea, and such-like places, but on the Hill it was unaccountable."*

> *Walter White, 1865.*
> *Eastern England from the Thames to the Humber.*

And then... the ague seemed to disappear. At the time, there was no consensus on the reasons.

"Dr Laver entered into an examination of the causes and the disappearance of the ague from Essex. In districts where the disease was fairly endemic, but from now which it had entirely disappeared, no drainage of swamps had been attempted, sanitary science was still unknown...

"Mr Greatheed, Mr White, Mr Crouch, Mr Ridley, and the President, in continuing the discussion, referred to the various theories (some wild enough) that had been devised to account for the decline of the ague - the use of sugar, the felling of woods, the increase of smoke of coals in the Thames neighbourhood owing to the steamers, drainage, and the general improvements in the modes of life and food were attended to - and it was pointed out that ague was generally most prevalent in the localities remote from civilizing influences."

The Essex Naturalist, Vol. II, 1888.

The ague was, in fact, a type of malaria spread by the mosquito, *Anopheles Maculipennis*. The low lying marshlands of the southern counties was its last stronghold in England. This is perhaps why the advice of 1854 *"... to avoid going out of doors after sunset, for an hour or so; and windows used to be closed about that period of the evening..."* appeared sound. It seems likely that this action kept the *"aguish miasma"* at bay, simply by keeping the mosquitoes out of the house at the time of the day they were particularly active.

THE KEY OF THE CITY OF LONDON...

In spite of the ague, Daniel Defoe decided to settle in Thurrock, in the parish of Chadwell; running a tile making factory by Tilbury Fort. Defoe was, therefore, particularly well qualified to write on local affairs. Tilbury Fort, as we know it today, had only just been completed when Defoe lived in the area.

> *"In the bottom of these marshes, and close to the edge of the river stands the strong fortress of Tilbury, called Tilbury Fort, which may justly be looked upon, as the key of the river of Thames, and consequently the key of the city of London. It is a regular fortification, the design of it, was a pentagon, but the water bastion as it would have been called, was never built. The esplanade of the fort is very large, and the bastions, the largest of England, the foundation is laid so deep, and piles under that, driven down two on end of one another, so far, till they were assured they were below the channel of the river... These bastions settled considerably at first, but they are now firm as the rocks of chalk they come from..."*
>
> *Daniel Defoe, 1724.*
> *A Tour Through the Whole Island of Great Britain.*

The 'bastions' were large triangular structures at each point of the pentagonal design of the fort. There were five of these on the original plans but the water bastion that was to stretch out into the Thames was never built. At low tide the foundations of the unbuilt bastion may still be seen jutting out into the Thames.

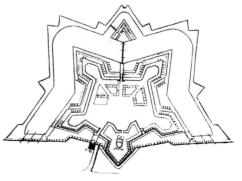

FROM THE GUNS...

The reach of the Thames between Defoe's home and Gravesend was a very active place for sea-going vessels. As well as playing its role in the defence of the city, Tilbury Fort also acted as gatekeeper for vessels departing from the great metropolis. Defoe could have watched the following activity within but a short walk from his home.

"The other thing for which this town (Gravesend) is worth notice, is, that all the ships which go out to sea from London, take their departure from hence; for here all outward-bound ships must stop, come to anchor, and suffer what they call second clearing, (viz.) here a searcher of the customs comes on board, looks over all the coquets or entries of the cargo, and may, if he pleases, rummage the whole loading, to see if there are no more goods that are entered; which however they seldom do, and besides being well treated on board, have generally three or five guns fired in honour to them when they go off.

When a merchant-ship comes down from London as soon as they come along the ships that are riding the road, the sentinel at the block-house, as they call it, on the Gravesend side fires his musket, which is to tell the pilot he must bring to; if he comes on, as soon as the ship passes broad side with the block-house, the sentinel fires again, which is as much as to say, why don't you bring to? if he drives a little farther, he fires a third time, and the language of that is bring to immediately, and let go your anchor, or we will make you. If the ship continues to drive down, and does not let go her anchor, the gunner of the fort is fetched, and he fires a piece of cannon though without a ball; and that is still a threat, though with some patience, and is to say, will you come to an anchor or won't you? If he still ventures to go on, by which he

gives them to understand he intends to run for it; then the
gunner fires again, and with a shot, and that shot is a signal
to the fortress over the river, (viz.) Tilbury Fort, and they
immediately let fly at the ship from the guns on the eastern
bastion and after from all the guns they can bring to bear
because they can reach her all they way unto the Hope, and
round the Hope-Point almost to Hole-Haven."

Daniel Defoe, 1724.
A Tour Through the Whole Island of Great Britain.

The "blockhouse" - based on a semicircular construction - to which
Defoe refers was a much earlier design of fortification than the then
newly built Tilbury Fort. The original blockhouse that stood on the Essex
side was incorporated in the design of the new Tilbury Fort; a second
blockhouse was to be found on the opposite bank of the river at
Gravesend, with three further downstream. It was hoped that they would
provide an impenetrable barrier to all intruders arriving by water.

FOR FEAR OF A FATAL COLLISION...

Another local landmark of national military importance was the nation's Gunpowder Magazine at Purfleet.

"From Erith we crossed the river to Purfleet. Its great chalk hill rose before us in this flat county like a Alp... We landed at the tremendous national Magazines of Gunpowder erected here in about the year 1762. Before that time they were at Greenwich which was thought to be too near our Capital. They consisted of five large parallel buildings each above a hundred and sixty feet long and fifty two wide, five feet thick, arched beneath the slated roof... All these building are surrounded at a distance with a lofty wall. In the two outmost is kept the power in small barrels, piled within wooden frames from the bottom to the roof and between the frames is a platform of planks that walkers may go in without fear of striking against any substance capable of emitting a spark. As a farther security, those who enter this dreadful place are furnished with goloshes, and a carters frock. Nothing of iron is admitted for fear of a fatal collision. The doors are of copper, the wheels of the barrows are of brass."

Thomas Pennant, 1784.
A Journey From London to Dover.

As well as the storage of gunpowder, the Purfleet Magazine was the site for testing *all* the gunpowder, produced by the various powder-makers, supplied to the Government. At Purfleet the gunpowder was tested, graded and transported to other Magazines across the kingdom.

EVERY ATOM OF POWDER...

At Purfleet, the possibility of explosions was ever-present, not due so much to the mere storage of gunpowder, but to the testing of the powder in such close proximity to the magazine.

"Since the disaster at Erith a great deal has been said as to the general management of the Government Magazines at Purfleet.. and the risks to which it is exposed.... Looking only at Purfleet as a mere place of storage for powder, there is no doubt that it is safe enough. As far as its storage is concerned there seems no chance of accident unless from 'unavoidable calamity'. What that calamity would be to England our readers may guess by bearing in mind that less than 50 tons exploded at Erith, and that Purfleet as a rule, stores 2,300... As a place for testing powder, Purfleet, with its tremendous magazines of explosives, seems objectionable."

The Engineer, 1864.

The explosion in the magazines at Erith occurred in October 1864. Neal (1992) records the effects, as reported in the *Kentish Independent,* of 8th October 1864 *"Thousands of pets have succumbed with fright, the mortality to canaries being very great. At the time of the explosion in the immediate neighbourhood, in every instance they dropped from their perches, and in very numerous cases expired. Parrots also, dropped into the bottom of their cages refusing to move for a quarter of an hour and declining to talk for a couple of hours."*

Although no major explosions occurred at Purfleet, other more minor calamitous events did. The following is recorded from some graffiti in the remaining magazine:

Morriss fell off a bay [with] a barrel on the top of him 29th March 1882 on a Wednesday

HIS PREFERENCE FOR 'BALLS'...

Concern for the safety of the magazine, was present from the start. The opinion of Benjamin Franklin, known for his experiments with lightning, was sought. However, at that time, Franklin was also known for his efforts in securing America's independence from colonial Britain - to the obvious disapproval of some. The political biases of the time openly influenced what should have been a purely scientific debate.

"In 1772 [Benjamin Franklin] was a member of a committee of the Royal Society to consider the best form of lighting rod for the powder magazines at Purfleet. A controversy arose as to whether the rods should terminate in balls or points. The King's attention was called to the matter. George III inquired what was the view of Franklin; and on being told that his political opponent was in favour of 'points', [the King] declared his preference for 'balls'."

J. Munro, 1890.
Pioneers of Electricity...
In Purfleet, compiled by I.G. Sparkes.

In pursuing America's independence Franklin obviously irritated many British opinion-makers. In an otherwise "measured" description of the Purfleet Magazine, Pennant (1784) wrote, *"A committee from the society was appointed, who determined on fixing conductors... These were on the principle advised by Doctor Benjamin Franklin. The very same Philosopher who living under the protection of our mild Government was secretly playing the incendiary, and too successfully inflaming the minds of our fellow subjects in America till the great explosion happened which for ever disunited us from our once happy Colonists."*

In 1777, lightning did strike one of the buildings. Pennant did, of course, take every opportunity to blame Franklin, *"... but the evil genius of the wily Philosopher stood victorious and our capital narrowly escaped subversion."*

30

AN IDEA EMBRAC'D IMMEDIATELY...

The Purfleet Power Magazine brought many great vessels to the shores of Thurrock. Captain Cook, who more than any other navigator added to our knowledge of the Pacific and Southern Oceans, also passed this way. Before embarking on his expedition of 1772, Cook's ship *Resolution* and his accompanying ship, *Adventure,* docked at Purfleet to load with gunpowder. The following incident was recorded by one of Cook's crew.

> *"Half a dozen of us had been walking in the country, and returning in the evening past the Governor of the Powder Magazine..., someone said, Lads, let us alarm the old Don a bit, by the whole party, and as there was three doors with bells, they were all instantly apply'd to most manfully, which soon brought out a most respectable looking gentleman, who seeing the party, begged to know what we wanted. He was answer'd we wish'd to see the curiosities of the place. He begged us to walk in, and we should see them; but someone said, No my old Buck, we only wanted to have the pleasure of seeing your face; and away we all ran."*

> *Midshipman John Elliot, 1772.*
> *In R.E. Bodle, 1980.*

This mild prank resulted in a complaint to the Admiralty. However, for the expedition, there were far greater worries in store. The *Adventure* returned from its voyage, prematurely, after losing some of its crew to cannibals - encountering more of a response than that received from *"old Buck",* at the start of their Journey.

Another ship calling at Purfleet, prior to its major voyage in 1787, was HMS *Bounty*. It is recorded that Captain Bligh went ashore at Purfleet to sign for the stores and munitions prior to sailing to the South Seas where the famous mutiny occurred.

TO BEAST AND CATTLE...

Returning to the blockhouse at Tilbury, Captain Talbot, in 1640, had his own local difficulties: various security risks, within the blockhouse, caused by the ferry. The "short ferry" or "cross ferry" from Tilbury to Gravesend was an important link between Essex and Kent. Just prior to Defoe's time, the ferry house on the Tilbury bank was actually within the fort - some distance east from the current landing stage. One can imagine the unsatisfactory nature of this arrangement.

"...there is a ferry house and ferry kept within the fort by the lord of the soil to his own benefit, through which passengers with their cattle and commodities (as though a common road and highway) do pass from Essex to Kent, by which means the fort not only lies open day and night to beasts and cattle, but the ordnance are liable to wrongs of ill disposed people."

Captain Talbot, 1640.
In J. R. Hayston, 1959.

In 1643 Captain Talbot also complained bitterly about the arrears of payment for his gunmen at the fort. I.G. Sparkes (1964), records that the House of Commons appear to have ordered that the ferry fees should be used to settle these payment arrears. So perhaps, for Captain Talbot, the inconvenience suffered by the arrivals and departures of the ferry did have its compensations.

DIFFERENCE WITH SOME WATERMEN...

Samual Pepys, the great diarist, and Secretary to the Admiralty, often passed this way, usually to review the ships moored off Thurrock's shores. The following entry illustrates the kind of altercations which might well have proven to be just too distracting for those whose duty it was to protect the river.

> *3rd August 1665. "...And anon came to the Blockhouse (Tilbury) over against Gravesend, where we stayed a great while - in a little drinking-house - sent back our coaches to Dagenhams. I by and by, by boat to Gravesend... and fetched them all over but the two saddle-horses that were to go with us, which could not be brought over in the horse-boat, the wind and tide being against us without towing. So we had some difference with some watermen, who would not tow them over under 20s - whereupon I swore to send one of them to sea, and will do it. Anon some others came to me and did it for ten."*
>
> *Samuel Pepys, 1665.*
> *The Diary Of Samual Pepys.*

A FROLIC TOOK US...

Although in the previous passage, Pepys travelled to the local area by carriage, more often he used the Thames. Before the days of paddle steamers the effect of the tides on such a journey cannot be overstated. If the tides were not kind to your journey, you didn't reach your destination, as Pepys discovered on one of his many visits to "the Hope" (the stretch of the Thames between East Tilbury and Stanford-le-Hope).

26th June 1664. "... and after dinner a frolic took us we would go this afternoon to the Hope. So my wife dressed herself, and with good victuals and drink we took the boat presently and, the tide with us, got down; but it was night and the tide spent by the time we got to Gravesend. So there we stopped but went not on shore; only Creed to get some cherries and sent a letter to the Hope where the fleet lies."

Samuel Pepys, 1664.
The Diary Of Samual Pepys.

AS WELL BY NIGHT AS BY DAY...

As recorded by Pepys, the journey between London and the Eastern counties was often made by river; indeed the "long ferry", operating between Gravesend and London, was an important link. Defoe, even in his day, was impressed by the number of people that travelled this route. It appears that the long ferry operated both night and day, probably - in the days before Steamers - to maximise the use of the tides.

"As I passed, I saw Gravesend from the hills... it is the town where the great ferry (as they call it) is kept up between London and East-Kent, is hardly credible what numbers of people pass here every tide, as well by night as by day, between this town and London. About 25 years ago one of these tilt-boats was cast away, occasioned by the desperate obstinacy and rudeness of the steersman or master, as they call him, who would tack again and stand over upon a wind, in the reach called Long-Reach, contrary to the advice and entreaties not of the passengers only but of his own rowers, who told him it blew a storm and she would founder; but he called them fools, bid the wind blow-devil (a rude sailor's proverb) the more wind the better the boat, till coming into the channel where the sea ran very high, he took in a wave, or a sea, as they call it, which run her down, and foundered her; and himself and three and fifty passengers were all drowned, only about five escaping by swimming"

Daniel Defoe, 1725.
A tour through the whole Island of Great Britain.

"Tilt-boats" were open sailing vessels, with a canvas cover called a "tilt" under which passengers could shelter from the worse of any weather. The tragedy to which Defoe refers was probably that of 1698 when a tilt-boat was lost along with 46 persons.

A THRONG OF PASSENGERS...

With the coming of the London-Tilbury railway, the importance of the "long ferry" declined, as people, even from east Kent, were using this railway line to travel to London. In 1865, as today, "commuters" appeared to undertake the prospect of their daily toil in the metropolis with little enthusiasm.

 *"Leaving Stanford by an early train the next morning, I came to Tilbury just as the steam ferry-boat arrived from Gravesend with a throng of passengers, mostly city men eager to reach their offices by ten o'clock. I walked down to the landing-stage to see them disembark; and whether it was my own holiday freedom from care, or that the signs of worldliness are most noticeable out of London, I could not but be struck by the general anxious expression of the faces, too firmly fixed to be removed by a 'blow' on the river or a night out of town. Among all that passed me as I stood leaning against the rail not one displayed a beaming eye or really happy feature."*

Walter White, 1865.
Eastern England from the Thames to the Humber.

SPIRITUAL AND BODILY COMFORT...

A well known local landmark for London bound commuters, whether by rail or river, was the church of St Clement. This once stood in splendid isolation on the marches of West Thurrock, with nothing but the marsh and sea wall between it and the Thames.

"Every traveller by the railway is struck by the singular position of the church, on the river bank, far away from the nearest house...it is separated from the village by... now... a comparative Eden, but then a swamp... It was built soon after the murder of Thomas Becket at Canterbury, for the spiritual and bodily comfort of pilgrims to his shrine...

[it was a]... folly or fashion of the period to erect a church on this natural halting place of their pilgrimage... before crossing the river to Kent. It is not unlikely that a refectory adjoined the church, with a dormitory for pilgrims waiting for favourable weather for crossing, which is not always safe or even possible, from its exposure to the prevailing south-west wind. The author has a lively recollection of the inconvenience, and, indeed, danger from crossing with his horse some years ago..."

Rev. William J.T. Palin, 1872.
More about Stifford and its Neighbourhood.

A BENIGN IMMENSITY...

In addition to Daniel Defoe, another author who settled in the area was Joseph Conrad. Conrad lived at Stanford-le-Hope, and was attracted to the area as, residing in the village was the family of his close friend, Captain Hope. Conrad was also a man of the sea and, no doubt, there was an attraction in living so close that *"interminable waterway"*, the Thames. Conrad and Hope spent many hours in their boat *"Nellie"* moored in the general area now known as Stanford Marshes. Conrad's writings evoke feelings that can still be experienced along this same stretch of the river.

"The Nellie, a cruising yawl, swung to her anchor without a flutter of the sails, and was at rest. The flood had made, the wind was nearly calm, and being bound down the river, the only thing for it was to come to and wait for the turn of the tide.

The sea-reach of the Thames stretched before us like the beginning of an interminable waterway. In the offing the sea and the sky were welded together without a joint, and in the luminous space the tanned sails of the barges drifting up with the tide seemed to stand still in red clusters of canvas sharply peaked, with gleams of vanishing spirits. A haze rested on the lower shores that ran out to sea in vanishing flatness. The air was dark above Gravesend, and farther back still seemed condensed into a mournful gloom, brooding motionless over the biggest, and the greatest, town on earth.

The Director of Companies was our captain and our host. We four affectionately watched his back as he stood in the bows looking seaward... Between us there was, as I have already said somewhere, the bond of the sea... We felt meditative, and fit for nothing but placid staring. The day was ending in a serenity of still and exquisite brilliance. The water shone pacifically; the sky, without a speck, was a benign immensity of unstained light; the very mists on the Essex marshes was like a gauzy and radiant fabric, hung from the wooded rises inland, and draping the low shores in diaphanous folds. Only the gloom to the west, brooding over the upper reaches, became more sombre every minute, as if angered by the approach of the sun.

And at last, in its curved and imperceptible fall, the sun sank low, and from glowing white changed to a dull red without rays and without heat, stricken to death by the touch of that gloom brooding over a crowd of men...

The sun set; the dusk fell on the stream, and the lights began to appear along the shore. The Chapman lighthouse, a three legged thing erect on a mud flat, shone strongly. Lights of ships moved in the fairway - a great stir of lights going up and down. And farther west on the upper reaches the place of the monstrous town was still marked ominously on the sky, a brooding gloom in sunshine, a lurid glare under the stars.

Joseph Conrad, 1902.
Heart of Darkness.

THE CHAPMAN LIGHTHOUSE

The Chapman Lighthouse, to which Conrad refers, stood, until recently, on the mud flats off Canvey Island.

The film *Apocalypse Now* - released 1979, starring Marlon Brando - itself described as *"... one of the most extraordinary war films ever made",* was based on Conrad's *Heart of Darkness.*

NOSING OUR WAY...

The Thames played a significant part in the recreational family life of Conrad. He and his wife, Jessie, would often don *"Mackintosh and gum-boots"* to embark on a Sunday expedition.

"Every Sunday he was well enough we would take a picnic lunch and join Mr Hope on a boating expedition. Fog or rain would not stop us. Often the mist was so low that we could see only a few yards and it was only such landmarks as haystacks on the banks of the narrow creeks and waterways that made it possible to tell of our whereabouts... most Sundays saw us dressed in Mackintosh and gum-boots, nosing our way in and out of the creeks that cut up the Essex Marshes, or feeling our way round the powder hulks that lay moored in the upper reaches of the Thames."

Jessie Conrad, 1935.
Joseph Conrad and his Circle.

FULL OF THINGS UNSPEAKABLE...

Not all home life was as "idyllic" for the Conrad's as exploring the creeks and waterways of Thurrock's marshes. The summer months appeared to cause some distress, caused by an influx of visitors. The following passage relates to their time in Ivy Walls, a farmhouse in Stanford-le-Hope, the Conrad's second home in the area.

"For several weeks I stayed on at the Essex Farm-House, enjoying my baby, but was greatly disturbed by the huge number of East-end Londoners imported by the farmer to pick the huge fields of peas, workers who were quartered in the big barn only a very short distance from my house... To have one hundred and eighty human beings living in such a confined space, drawing water from the only pump, right at one's back door, was a situation that called for all my tact and not a little endurance... Narrow wooded planks divided the men and boys from the women and children, and the fairway or channel down the centre was full of things unspeakable. There was a fair amount of illness among the children..."

Jessie Conrad, 1935.
Joseph Conrad and his Circle.

Whilst the above influx must have proved a disruption to a generally quiet village life, it does provide a good documentation of the accommodation that were usual for this migratory workforce.

Jessie Conrad later described how the workers, after assisting with the harvesting of the Essex fields, would then move to the hop-fields of Kent.

THE WINDING RIVER TURNED...

Another writer to have some associations with the area was Charles Dickens. Whilst Dickens never lived in the area, he often passed through Thurrock; travelling from his home in Kent, across the short ferry, to Tilbury and then on to London by train. Thus, Dickens, as Defoe before him, and Conrad after, wrote about the area from personal experience. In the following passage Pip and his companions travel down the Thames from London.

[Departing from Temple Stairs]... "Our plan was this. The tide, beginning to run down at nine, and being with us until three, we intended still to creep on after it had turned, and row against it until dark. We should then be well in those long reaches below Gravesend, between Kent and Essex, where the river is broad and solitary, where the water-side inhabitants are very few, and where lone public-houses are scattered here and there, of which we could choose one for a resting-place...

The tide ran strong, I took care to lose none of it, and our steady stroke carried us on thoroughly well. By imperceptible degrees, as the tide ran out, we lost more and more of the nearer woods and hills, and dropped lower and lower between the muddy banks, but the tide was yet with us when we were off Gravesend... And soon the tide began to slacken, and the craft lying at anchor to swing... we kept under the shore, as much out of the tide as we could, standing carefully off from low shallows and mud-banks...

We got ashore among some slippery stones... and looked about. It was like my own marsh country, flat and monotonous, and with a dim horizon; while the winding river turned and turned, and everything else seemed to stand still. For, now, the last of the fleet of ships was round the last low point we had headed... and a little squat shoal-lighthouse on open piles, stood crippled in the mud on stilts and crutches; and slimy stakes stuck out of the mud, and slimy stones stuck out of the mud, and red landmarks and tidemarks stuck out of the mud, and an old landing stage and an old roofless building slipped into the mud, and all about us was stagnation and mud.

We pushed off again and made what way we could. It was much harder work now, but Herbert and Startop persevered, and rowed, and rowed, and rowed, until the sun went down. By that time the river had lifted us a little, so that we could see over the bank. There was the red sun, on the low level of the shore, in a purple haze, fast deepening into black; and there was the solitary flat marsh; and far away there were the rising grounds, between which and us there seemed to be no life, save here and there in the foreground a melancholy gull.

As the night was falling fast... our course was to lie by at the first lonely tavern we could find. So they plied their oars once more, and I looked out for anything like a house. Thus we held on, speaking little, for four or five dull miles... At length we descried a light and a roof, and presently afterwards ran alongside a little causeway made of stones that had been picked up hard-by. Leaving the rest in the boat, I stepped ashore, and found the light to be in a window of a public-house. It was a dirty place enough, and I daresay not unknown to smuggling adventurers; but there was a good fire in the kitchen, and there were eggs and bacon to eat, and various liquors to drink.

[Pip and his companions decided to rest for the night] I lay

down with the greater part of my clothes on, and slept well for a few hours. When I awoke, the wind had risen, and the sign of the house (the Ship) was creaking and banging about with noises that startled me. Rising softly... I looked out of the window. It commanded the causeway where we had hauled up our boat, and, as my eyes adapted themselves to the light of the clouded moon, I saw two men looking into her. They passed by under the window, looking at nothing else, and they did not go down to the landing place, which I could discern to be empty, but struck across the marsh in the direction of the Nore."

Charles Dickens, 1861.
Great Expectations.

Although in the following section of the book, *The Widening Thames*, R. H. Goodsall, was referring to the Kent marshes, his recommendations hold equally well for the Essex marshes: *"I recommend any who are unfamiliar with this fascinating... backwater first to read again their Dickens, particularly Great Expectations, and then with map in hand and perhaps a camera or sketching pad, set forth on a journey of exploration. They will be richly rewarded".* As Goodsall recommends, it is worth setting forth on such a journey of exploration, to tease out the clues, in the landscape, that Dickens has left.

In *Great Expectations*, Dickens records that Pip and his companions passed Gravesend, travelling downstream - this puts them firmly along Thurrock's shoreline.

A short while after reaching Gravesend, Dickens makes reference to the course of the river, *"... the winding river turned and turned"* - Indeed, just below Gravesend the river does turn sharply north into The Hope (at East Tilbury) and then sharply east (at Stanford marshes): this puts the travellers in the general area of Stanford Marshes. The *"... little squat shoal-lighthouse...crippled in the mud on stilts and crutches"* is a reference the Mucking lighthouse (similar in style to the Chapman Lighthouse to which Conrad referred). Mucking lighthouse was in fact located in what is now Stanford - at one time the Mucking Parish owned that portion of land in the marshlands of Stanford where the lighthouse was sighted.

We can be sure that the travellers landed on the Essex bank, as Pip records that it was *"like my own marsh country"* [Pip's own country was Kent]. After this brief respite they continued to row against the tide for *"... four or five dull miles"*. This puts the public house quite a way downstream from the Mucking lighthouse. Although only about three miles downstream (but the travellers were rowing *against* the tide), we arrive at The Lobster Smack on the shores of Canvey Island - this appears to be the public house to which Dickens refers as the "Ship". Claims by other hostelries to be the "Ship" are unfounded.

The Lobster Smack still exists and is to be found on the western tip of Canvey Island. Whilst this moves somewhat outside the immediate locality, by water it is but a few yards away from Thurrock.

This stretch of the river along Thurrock's shoreline described in *Great Expectations* is the same stretch of river described by Conrad some 40 years later.

A SOLITARY TUMBLE-DOWN INN...

The Lobster Smack does not only get a mention by Dickens; it is more convincingly identified by the author Robert Buchanan.

"...There stood in the loneliest part of Canvey Island, at the mouth of the Thames, a solitary tumble-down inn called the Lobster Smack.

Its landlord was a certain Job Endell, who had once been a deep sea mariner and, if reports did not greatly belie him, a savage sea-dog and pirate; its patrons, few and far between, were such fisherman, bargees, lighterman, and riverside characters as were driven in their various vessels by stress of weather or freaks of the tide into the little muddy haven close to the inn door. From time to time the little inn resounded with the merriment of such wayfarers, but as a rule it was as deserted as its surroundings, and the aforesaid Job Endell was the lonely Monarch of all he surveyed.

Now and then, however, Job had the privilege of entertaining a stray visitor from London, attracted thither by the choices of fishing in the river or sea-bird shooting in the creeks along the sea-wall; and at the time when our story opens two such visitors... were occupying the only two habitable guest chambers in the inn...

...Gazing through the open window, through which the air stole warm and heavy with the scent of sea-grass and weed, Somerset saw the creek filled almost to overflowing with the spring tide and glancing like mother-of-pearl in the brightening moon rays. Black against the sky loomed the silhouette of the little yawl, now floating and swinging at anchor, and out beyond, in the shadow for the most part, but

with here and there a glimmer of reflected moonlight, lay the Great River. All was completely still, save for the occasional cry of a curlew passing onward to join the flocks at rest on the marshes till low water. Brighter and brighter grew the moon, rising higher in the heavens, and shedding further ablutions of silver light, till all the skies seemed flooded with her beams, while the shimmering tide crept closer and closer...

...Standing in the shadows of the old inn, Somerset looked across the creek towards the river. Far away across it dim red lights were twinkling on the coast of Kent. Shadows went and came. Then there was a deep sea sound from the distance and a black tug went by, churning up the phosphorescence with its paddle-wheels and dragging behind it the blacker shadow of a great ship. Somerset stood and listened, as the sound grew fainter and fainter, dying away up the river."

Robert Buchanan, 1901.
Andromeda: An Idyll of the Great River.

LIKE A SHOWER OF PEARLS...

The following description of the local marshlands evokes the sentiments of Dickens, Conrad and Buchanan:

"North of Tilbury, and away to the eastward along the Essex shore, stretches a strange, level country netted with winding streams. As the tide runs out, the little ditches send down runnels of clear water. Charles Dickens was always fascinated by this region; but, strangely enough, his works have given everybody a false impression of the whole marsh country. People think of slime, and darkness, and poisonous exhalations, and an atmosphere of horror and crime. They think the faces of hunted convicts and the grim night-scenes in which Joe Gargery and his pet took part; but at certain times of the year the marshes are really cheerful the clear streams glitter in the morning sun, and the larks sing their hearts out high up in the air. The multitudinous notes fall around you from the shining heights like a shower of pearls, and for miles the eye is met by a blaze of colour and dazzling glitter. The ragworts spread in blinding sheets of yellow; the purple stars of the mallow peep modestly out from the coarse grass; and amid all the riot of sound and colour the peaceful cattle stand, and give a sense of homely companionship to the scene. When the tide flows, the river slips into the channels and the tiny runnels of spring water are driven back to their sources; the ditches fill and overflow; the fishes, in many cases, catch their prey within a yard of where the cattle were feeding; and the grass becomes impregnated by the tide. It is this daily advance of the brackish flood that makes the marshes so valuable as grazing grounds. The cattle eagerly tear at the salty grass, and its nutritive qualities are so great that it is sometimes found that a whole herd turned out on the marshes within a week or two weigh on the average half a

*stone more than they did when they first fed on the saltings.
In winter, truly, the marshes are bleak and inhospitable; but
in the soft, rich mud of the ditches the wild-fowl swarm, and
the sportsmen have good times when the weather is frosty. A
man who is not greedy and who will be content with a very
moderate bag, can hardly find a better place for exciting sport
than within these northern saltings. Sometimes a redshank
starts up, whistling desperately, and goes off down wind until
the charge stops him; the ringed plovers cower low in the
ditch, and shoot along under the bank with steady, level flight,
until they are forced to sweep out over the grass and give the
gunner his chance.*

*J. Runciman.
Gravesend to the Nore, Chapter XII, The Thames, from
Source to the Sea. (In) The Royal River.*

WE TRANSYLVANIAN NOBLES...

Whilst the writings of Dickens, Conrad and Buchanan present a reliable record of the local landscape, the historical evidence regarding another local character is less convincing. *"Dracula"*, the Victorian gothic masterpiece by Bram Stoker, has some local associations.

"At Purfleet, on a by-road I came across just such a place as seemed to be required, and where was displayed a dilapidated notice that the place was for sale. It is surrounded by a high wall, of ancient structure, built of heavy stones, and has not been repaired for a large number of years. The closed gates were of heavy old oak and iron, all eaten with rust.

The estate is called Carfax... It contains in all some twenty acres, quite surrounded by the solid stone wall above mentioned. There are many trees on it, which make it in places gloomy, and there is a deep, dark-looking pond or small lake, evidently fed by some springs, as the water is clear and flows away in a fair-sized stream. The house is very large and of all periods back, I should say, to medieval times, for one part is of stone immensely thick, with only a few windows high up and heavily barred with iron. It looks like part of a keep, and is close to an old chapel or church. I could not enter it, as I had not the key of the door, leading to it from the house, but I have taken with my Kodak views of it from various points. The house has been added to, but in a very straggling way, and I can only guess at the moment of ground it covers, which must be very great. There are but a few houses close at hand one being a very large house only recently added to and formed into a private lunatic asylum.

When I had finished he [Dracula] said:- "I am glad that it is old and big, I myself am of an old family and to live in a new

*house would kill me... I rejoice that there is a chapel of old
times. We Transylvanian nobles love not to think that our
bones may be amongst the common dead. I seek not gaiety nor
mirth, not the bright voluptuousness of much sunshine and
sparkling waters which please the young and gay. I am no
longer young and my heart, through the weary years of
mourning over the dead, is not attuned to mirth."*

Bram Stoker, 1897.
Dracula.

Was Dracula's Purfleet residence inspired by Stoker's personal
knowledge of the area, laced with poetic license... or was it pure
imagination? Perhaps we shall never know.

There is a strong local opinion that Purfleet House, built by Samuel
Whitbread - and used as his main residence in 1791 - could have been
the inspiration for Carfax House with the Purfleet Magazine providing the
basis for the lunatic asylum. And the Botany gardens might have fitted
well the description of the grounds of the Carfax Estate. With regard to
the *"... springs",* and the *"... fair size stream",* certainly there were local
springs, rising from the chalk, and the Mardyke flowed nearby.

Whilst there is no record of Stoker
visiting Purfleet, we do know that
Purfleet was a popular attraction for
the day visitor from London; we also
know that, in the late 1890s, Stoker
worked at London's Royal Lyceum
Theatre. So, perhaps the setting
was based on more than pure
imagination.

MINGLED FAILURES AND SUCCESSES...

ovelists were not the only writers associated with Thurrock: another resident who achieved international acclaim, through his scientific writings, was the notable Victorian biologist - and contemporary of Charles Darwin - Alfred Russel Wallace. Whilst Charles Darwin is credited for shaking the scientific world with his theory of evolution, Wallace developed this theory independently of - and at the same time as - Darwin. To this day however, Darwin has received the credit, mainly as a consequence of being the first author to publish his works. In 1859, the influence of Darwin's book *"Origin of Species..."* was profound. Wallace and Darwin were scientific companions; presenting joint papers at scientific meetings, and corresponding with each other about their theories and latest works. When Wallace moved to Grays - at a time when there were many letters flowing between him and Darwin - he was most enthusiastic about the grounds he had acquired. The following description captures that enthusiasm.

"In the following year, 1871, I found near the village of Grays, on the Thames, twenty miles from London, a picturesque old chalk-pit which had been disused so long that a number of large elms and a few other trees had grown up in its less precipitous portions. The chalk here was capped by about twenty feet of Thanet sand and Pleistocene gravel, and from the fields at the top there was a beautiful view over Erith to the Kent hills and down a reach of the Thames to Gravesend, forming a most attractive site for a house. After some difficulty I obtained a lease for ninety-nine years of four acres, comprising the pit itself, an acre of the field on the plateau above, and about an equal amount of undulating cultivable ground between the pit and the lane which gave access to it. I had to pay seven pounds an acre rent, as the owner could not sell it, and though I thought it very dear, as so much of it was unproductive, the site was so picturesque,

and had such capabilities of improvement, that I thought it would be a fair investment. As there was a deep bed of rough gravel on my ground and there were large cement works at Grays, I thought it would be economical to build of concrete, and I found an architect of experience, Mr. Wonnacott, of Farnham, who made the plans and specifications, while I myself saw that the gravel was properly washed. In order to obtain water in ample quantity for building and also for garden and other purposes, I had a well sunk about a hundred feet into a water-bearing stratum of the chalk, and purchased a small iron windmill with a two-inch force pump to obtain the water. I made two small concrete ponds in the garden-one close to the windmill - and had a large tank at the top of a low tower to supply house water. My friend Geach, the mining engineer whom I had met in Timor and Singapore, was now at home, and took an immense interest in my work. He helped me to find the windmill - the only one that we could discover in any of the engineering shops in London - and the well being completed he and I, with the assistance of my gardener, did all the work of fitting the pump at the bottom of the well with connecting-rods and guides up the windmill, which also we erected and set to work ourselves. As the windmill had no regulating apparatus, and, then the wind became strong revolved far too rapidly and even bent the connecting rod, I attached to the ends of the iron vanes, pieces of plate iron, about a foot square, fixed at right angles to the line of motion. These acted as brakes as soon as the revolution became moderately rapid, but had little effect, when it was slow; and the arrangement worked very well. With the help of another labourer I also myself laid down 1½ inch galvanized water pipes to the house, with branches and taps where required in the garden. I also built concrete walls *round the acre of ground at top, the part facing south about nine feet high for fruit trees, the rest about five feet; and also laid out the garden, planted mounds for shelter, made a winding road from below, which, when the shrubs had grown up, became exceedingly picturesque; and helped to sift out hundreds of cubic yards of gravel to improve the land for the kitchen garden. All this work was immensely interesting, and I have seldom enjoyed myself more thoroughly, especially as my friend Geach was a continual visitor, was always ready with his help and advice, and took as much interest in the works as I did myself. We got into the house in March, 1872, and I began to take that pleasure in gardening and especially in growing uncommon and interesting as well as beautiful plants, which in various places, under many difficulties and with mingled failures and successes, has been a delight and solace to me ever since."*

Alfred Russel Wallace, 1905.
My Life: A Record of Events and Opinions. Vol. II.

ITS DEEP AND PICTURESQUE RAVINE...

Whilst Alfred Russel Wallace showed particuar affection for his own house and gardens, there were other fine residences in the area around Grays.

> *"Among the principal residences, at present, are Belmont Castle (a handsome modern erection by Zachary Button, of Ford Place, Stifford...); Duvals (a sort of Eagle's Nest...); the Elms (a fairy land, with its deep and picturesque ravine and pleasure grounds); Grays Hall... (commanding exquisite views of the river and opposite coast of Kent)..."*
>
> *Rev. William J.T. Palin, 1871.*
> *Stifford and its Neighbourhood: Past and Present.*

The caveat *"at present"* indicated that Palin was convinced that the area was ripe for development; and that there were to be built more *"principal residences"*. Indeed at the time Palin was writing this, Wallace was building his own principal residence on land between The Elms and Grays Hall. Wallace's house is still standing, as is Grays Hall. The Elms, that *"fairy land with its deep and picturesque ravine and pleasure grounds"* is recorded as having been demolished in 1979 - the grounds are now occupied by a school.

GENIUS OF CAPABILITY BROWN...

One of the other *"principal residences"* in the area was Belhus, a magnificent Tudor building, in Aveley. The mansion was matched only by the splendour of its grounds, which were landscaped by Lancelot *"Capability"* Brown.

"Bel House, has all the features of a baronial mansion, with Battlements, turrets, and small windows of the structure which prevailed in the reign of Henry VIII. It has also a very fine and extensive southern view over the river Thames, and into Kent. The apartments of the house... are very magnificent, and ornamented with stained glass,.... The Library, besides containing a very excellent assortment of the classics... is furnished with an invaluable collection of British antiquities, general, and county history... The park and grounds are extensive, and well laid out, by the genius of Capability Brown; and the scenery is grand and picturesque."

D. Hughson, 1809.
Circuit of London, Vol. 6.

Belhus became derelict. In 1956 it was reported that it would cost £35,000 to restore; the mansion was soon demolished.

THE OLD SHRIVELLED HANDS...

Belhus has its own history and, in common with many grand houses, at least one ghost:

"I have slept in old castles and houses, some rooms in which were said to be haunted, and the last of them... was at the ancient and interesting seat of my friend Sir Thomas Barrett Lennard, at Belhus, in Essex. The form of an old female domestic is reputed there as occasionally seen haunting the galleries and stairs between the rooms. Somehow or other, one night, perhaps a cold one, she had taken it into her head to seat herself by the fire in the bedroom in which more recently I slept, and was there beheld by one whose word I do not doubt, though she admitted to having been so frightened in her passage through the room by a seated figure, 'the old shrivelled hands resting on the knees,' that she stayed not for further observation, question and reply, but hastened at once to reach more agreeable quarters.

In the red glare of the dying embers, or by the fitful beam of an expiring lamp, the old chair in that bedroom of the hospitable house of my kind friend, has pressed itself on my gaze in connexion with the story of the ghost, but I never saw it filled by another form than my own, nor do I wish to see that chair or any other occupied by a visitant from beyond the grave."

Hon. Grantly Berkeley, 1866.
Life and Recollections.

57

BY A GOTHIC TEMPLE...

Belmont Castle in Grays was also one of the larger country estates in the area.

"Belmont Castle, most delightfully situated, one mile from Grays, was the property and residence of the late Zachariah Button, Esq. who finished it in an early style of Gothic architecture. The building contains, besides other convenient apartments, a circular neatly finished room, called the Round Tower, from whence there are the most delightful prospects of the river Thames, of the shipping for many miles, and of the rich Kentish inclosures, to the hills beyond the great Dover road. An elegant drawing room, with circular front highly encircled; a cheerful entrance hall, finished with Gothic mouldings, niches for figures or lamps, and paved with stone, and black marble dots... The large and very excellent kitchen garden is incompassed with lofty walls, clothed and planted with a choice selection of the best fruit trees, and a capital hot-house. Surrounding the house, are the pleasure grounds, which are beautifully and tastefully disposed, and ornamented with very valuable forest trees, shrubs, and plants, terminating towards the west by a Gothic temple, and towards the east by an orchard and paddock. There are two approaches to the house, the one by the neat brick Gothic lodge, through the great south lawn, from the road between West Thurrock and Grays; and the other from the village of Stifford, by the north lawn."

D. Hughson, 1809.
Circuit of London, vol. 6.

58

THE MONSTROUS RED-BRICK PILE...

Some local architecture was greeted less enthusiastically. The following passage can only be a reference to the Tilbury Hotel, which stood on the north bank of the Thames.

> *"Between the houses of Gravesend and the monstrous red-brick pile on the Essex shore the ship is surrendered fairly to the grasp of the river. That hint of loneliness, that soul of the sea which had accompanied her as far as the Lower reach, abandons her at the turn of the first bend above."*
>
> *Joseph Conrad, 1906.*
> *The Mirror of the Sea.*

Not all opinion was as damning as that of Conrad's: some years later a local writer (Loftus, 1949) proclaimed that *"... the massive pile of the Tilbury Hotel had a friendly look to the passengers returning to England after years abroad... It was, I think, to the Thames, what the Statue of Liberty is to New York Bay".* The Tilbury Hotel opened on the same day as the Docks, in April 1886. It was burned out in 1944, a casualty of enemy action.

AND TALK WITH 'DEEP THINKERS'...

Not all large residences were notable only for their presence in the landscape. Moore Place, a 17th century farmhouse at Stanford-le-Hope, was established as a social "Colony" by Captain Petavel, where like-minded people were experimenting with social reform.

"A Strange and Novel Deep Thinkers' Home at Stanford-le-Hope... Here people interested in social reform are received and can mix and talk with 'deep thinkers' who have evolved a means of doing away with unemployment and its attending evils."

Black & White Magazine, 1910.

Sympathetic visitors were invited to stay and to promote the ideals of the colony. The colony was intended to be self-supporting, expecting its guests to be vegetarian and non-smokers - although some tolerance was afforded to guests: it is recorded that a guest *"...would not be summarily ejected if he occasionally indulged himself in 'the fragrant weed' or fortified himself with a chop or a steak."*

MOORE PLACE SOCIAL . . . . . .
SETTLEMENT AND GUEST HOUSE,
Stanford-le-Hope.   Essex.

Station—Stanford-le-Hope. Distance One Mile.
Carriages meet all trains.

GUIDE TO VISITORS

With Pictures from an illustrated article in "Black and White" from photos by Messrs. Chas. J. L. Clarke.

TO INTELLIGENTLY APPRECIATE...

In spite the laudable aims of the Moore Place Colony, of promoting individual freedom, some difficulties were apparently encountered, when the freedoms of the few interfered with the freedoms of the many.

"It is intended that freedom, not regulation, be the rule of the place. People will co-operate, as among friends and people staying for a holiday, who want anything but mathematically precise arrangements. The regulations made are an irreducible minimum, but visitors are requested to intelligently appreciate their necessity, not only because the helpers are voluntary, but because a Colony of this kind has its harsh critics, especially among people having similar but not identical ideas, ready to find fault.

Inconvenience arises through people being late to retire. Lights are therefore put out in the common rooms at 10.15, and at 10.30 on Saturdays, and the house is shut.

As trouble is given by people being late for breakfast, the rule is made that if anyone does not come down by 9 o'clock breakfast is taken to their room and an extra charge of 2d. a day, or 9d a week is made.

During the Colony's first year the above rules were not made - it was a year of experiment. The result was inconvenience to guests as well as to co-operators."

Guide to Visitors, c. 1911.
Moore Place Social Settlement and Guest House.

FRESH AND EFFICIENT HELPERS...

Some time after its opening, it appears that whilst the "thinking" guests of Moore Place were many, there was less response from guests able to make a practical contribution to the running of the Colony. In attempting to gain more support, the vegetarian "cause" became more prominent.

"The Vegetarian and Social Colony at Stanford-le-Hope feels that it has not had the support it should have had from Vegetarians, and if they do not help it, it may cease to be a Vegetarian Colony...

...instead of getting useful co-operators, we got people who, though very nice and very interesting, have not got the qualifications to be practically helpful; one by one they went off. I suppose that it is only human nature that those people who did not do for the place what they might have done went away blaming the place, and not themselves...

We have at last got fresh and efficient helpers, and fortunately people very well inclined towards vegetarianism, so the Colony is not yet lost to the cause, but if vegetarians continue to lend us no assistance of any kind, it certainly may be!"

J. W. Petaval, 1911.
Vegetarian Messenger.

Ultimately the project never reached the aspirations of its founder: Captain Petavel still pursuing his ideals, went to India. Moore Place was later acquired by the *"Wayfarers' Benevolent Association";* it was subsequently sold and demolished to give way to "development" of a different kind.

DESCENDS TO A DEPTH...

In the late 1800s, Thurrock was not only graced with fine residences and notable people, the very land itself had provoked considerable interest: specifically the underground caves. Known as 'deneholes', and entered only by a vertical shaft, these caverns are still to be found in Hangman's Wood, adjacent to the Daneholes Roundabout on the A1013.

"Hangman's Wood is a small wood partly in the parish of Little Thurrock and partly in Orsett. At the south of this wood... are traces of numerous pits...

The formation of such are still comparatively perfect... A perpendicular shaft of about 3 feet in diameter, and like that of an ordinary well, descends to a depth of about 75 or 80 feet. At the foot of each shaft one each side large chambers are cut out of the chalk.

The surmises as to the purpose for which these pits were dug are conflicting, some persons inclining to the belief that they were workings for chalk; but this theory, it is thought, can scarcely be upheld in the face of so many shafts so near each other; for, had the object been to procure chalk, the chambers would have been worked into galleries... Another theory is that they were made for granaries or storing-places, and this seems to be the most applicable, for the chambers are perfectly dry, and access to them so difficult, that such a supposition appears to be a reasonable solution of their origin."

R. Lloyd Williams, 1872.
(In) More About Stifford and its Neighbourhood.

SUBTERRANEAN CAMERA WORK...

The interest in this "discovery" led to much exploration, excitement and activity.

"On Saturday morning the explorers were early on the ground, and Mr Arnold Spiller... kindly undertook the task of 'photographing a Denehole' a feat of subterranean camera work presenting very special difficulties... For the light, magnesium burning in oxygen was employed; two quart bottles of the gas and two feet of the metal in the form of ribbon...

The visitors on Saturday were very numerous, particularly during the afternoon, a number of ladies being included in the company... The large majority of those present descended into one or other of the excavations, and the little wood in the fields was the scene of unusual animation... The descent into No 3 pit was effected with comfort, a chair-like seat being used from which it was impossible to fall...

Enriched by plans, bones, insects, and other geological specimens the party returned to Grays shortly after six o'clock, and set down to a capital knife and fork tea, admirably served by Mr. Cummings at the Kings Arms Hotel."

Essex Field Club, 1892.
Journal of Proceedings at Ordinary, Field, and Other Events For February 1883 to January 1887.

A CURIOUS FEATURE...

Although the discovery of the deneholes led to much activity, their exact purpose was a matter of some debate.

> *"A curious feature of the district is the occurrence of the Dane Holes, as they are called by the country people, and of which antiquarians form such different ideas, I believe they are simply excavations to obtain chalk for lime-burning; subsequently, however, used for other purposes, as for burial in the Roman period. I have opened one full of Roman burial vases crushed by the fall of the roof, but from which I extracted one nearly perfect, containing the bones of a female and a child, with Bronze armlets, and a spindle whorl of lead. I have never seen in them evidence of occupation as dwellings or stores. The mode of obtaining chalk by this mode of sinking wells down to the chalk, and then driving tunnels, is now in operation."*

Richard Meeson, 1871.
(In) Stifford and its Neighbourhood: Past and Present.

A HITHERTO UNKNOWN CHAPTER...

Other authorities, at the time, believed that the deneholes were far more significant than mere chalk excavations. Although Alfred Russel Wallace moved from Grays in 1876, members of the Essex Field Club tracked him down to seek his opinion on the significance of the deneholes.

Frith Hill,
Godalming.

Oct. 8th 1883.

Dear Mr Meldola.

In reply to your letter asking for my opinion as to the advisability of an exploration of the Daneholes at Grays, I have no hesitation in saying that, and likely to lead to very interesting results. Having resided at Grays for some years, and being well acquainted with the general aspect of the surrounding country, as well as with the position and main features of the Daneholes themselves, and having Mr Holmes' excellent account of the explorations already made at Grays and elsewhere, it appears to me in the highest degree probably that these curious excavations were originally granaries or stone-cellars, and that they indicate the site of ancient villages of some unknown but probably prehistoric epoch. Their thorough examination may therefore reveal a hitherto unknown chapter in the history of our island. Looking at the great number of these very deep and narrow shafts crowed together in such a small space and leading to symmetrically excavated chambers which do not usually... communicate with each other, and considering further that chalk and flint are to be obtained close to the surface within a distance of about a mile, and that all ancient excavations for the purpose of obtaining these substances differ radically from Daneholes in all their essential features - the suggestion that they are mere chalk or flint pits, and that therefore no exploration is necessary, appears to me to be quite on par with that celebrated explanation of the glacial striae, as being mere scratches and ruts produced by cart-wheels of the native inhabitants.

Believe me,

Yours very faithfully,

Alfred R. Wallace

Alfred R. Wallace, 1883.
Essex Field Club Journal, vol. iv. 1885-86.

The deneholes never really revealed *"... a hitherto unknown chapter in the history of our island...",* and the significance attached by Wallace was never proven. The earlier, more mundane, explanation was correct: the deneholes were simply excavations for chalk - but an interesting episode nevertheless.

It is not surprising that the purpose of the deneholes were that of chalk extraction, as chalk had been excavated for agricultural purposes for many years; for the local land, and for other areas, where heavy clay soil predominated.

OF ALL THE ROADS...

Whilst some people were debating the origin of the chalk caverns, others were encountering the effects of chalk quarrying. The following extract presents a severe indictment of some of Thurrock's roads; the traveller's journey not being made any easier by the transportation of chalk from Thurrock to other farming areas of Essex.

"Of all the roads that ever disgraced this Kingdom, in the very ages of barbarism none ever equalled that from Billericay to the King's Head at Tilbury. It is for near 12 miles so narrow, that a mouse cannot pass by any carriage; I saw a fellow creep under his wagon to assist me to lift, if possible, my chaise over a hedge. The rutts are of an incredible depth - and a pavement of diamonds might as well be sought for as a quarter. The trees every where over-grow the road, so that it is totally impervious to the sun, except at a few places: And to add to all the infamous circumstances, which concur to plague a traveller, I must not forget eternally meeting with chalk-wagons; themselves frequently stuck fast, till a collection of them are in the same situation, that twenty or thirty horses may be tacked to each, to draw them out one by one."

Arthur Young,
King's Head, (West) Tilbury, 1767.
A Six Weeks' Tour Through the Southern Counties of England and Wales, 1772.

TUMULTS AND OTHER DISORDERS...

Although the journey to Thurrock may have been arduous, was it ever worthwhile? There are some clues: it looks as though Thurrock was infamous for its informal "gatherings".

> *"It being represented to this Court that many loose, idle and disorderly persons have for several years past used and accustomed themselves to assemble and meet together at several pretended fairs held in this Country, not warranted by Law, that is to say, Aveley fair, Bulphan fair, ... Corringham fair, Fobbing fair, Great Warley fair, Little Thurrock fair, West Thurrock fair, South Ockendon fair, Stanford-Le-Hope fair, Stifford fair, West Tilbury fair.... Some of which fairs are continued for several days and great numbers of people stay there not only all days, but to very late hours in the night, and many unlawful games and plays, besides drinking and other debaucheries are encouraged and carried on under pretence of meeting at such fairs to the great increase of vice and immorality and to the debauching and ruin of servants, apprentices and other unwary people and many riots, tumults and other disorders are occasioned thereby. For the preventing of all such mischiefs and irregularities for the future, it is thought fit and ordered by this court that the said fairs be henceforth absolutely suppressed."*

> *Quarter Sessions Order Book, 20 April 1762.*
> *In A.F.J. Brown, English History From Essex Sources.*

Although this was recorded some 60 years after Defoe left the district, we can only speculate whether Defoe himself ever indulged in *"... drinking and other debaucheries".* The evidence suggests that whilst he may have *observed* the *"vice and immorality"* of local fairs, he probably did not partake: he was somewhat critical of such behaviour.

69

A CALAMITOUS CONFLAGRATION...

Some years later the local entertainment still often got a little rowdy, especially on November the fifth.

"But as evening came on the streets were alive with minor pyrotechnical displays; squibs, crackers, and other fireworks were flying about in all directions. Lighted tar barrels were rolled about and the efforts of the police were for a time unavailing. But the climax was reached when it was reported that a house down the lower part of High-Street had been set alight by a tar barrel. The report turned out to be only too true, and the Fire Brigade were called out. They appeared on the scene in a short space of time, and to their exertions must be attributed the fact that a calamitous conflagration did not ensue. The whole of one side of the house, in the occupation of Mr W. Roberts, was burnt away; and unfortunately he is not insured. At midnight matters got to such a pitch that the constables on duty were compelled to draw their staves, and they had such a rough experience for some time, but ultimately succeeded in clearing the streets."

Grays and Tilbury Gazette, Nov. 1891.

As recent as 1957 local residents could remember earlier days when *"... Bargemen on bonfire night used to get a barrel of tar, set it on fire, and roll the blazing mass down the slope of the Old High Street."*[1] To this day a strikingly similar tradition is upheld on the streets of Ottery St Mary in Devon.

---

[1] Bannister, *The Recollections of a Septuagenarian.* 1957.

A LICENCE FOR LICENTIOUSNESS...

Even on occasions other than Bonfire Night, the local entertainment still seemed lively. In a description of Grays Thurrock, the Rev. Palin records:

> *"The number of public houses in this little port-town strikes outsiders more than the licensing bench at Orsett. A writer in Once a Week, Feb. 24 1866, says of Grays, 'for its size it contains more than any other town in England'. It is well known that many of these are conducted in a way contrary to the letter and spirit of the licence... With these a licence reads a licence for licentiousness..."*
>
> *Rev. William J. T. Palin, 1872.*
> *More About Stifford and its Neighbourhood.*

It is unknown whether the Rev. Palin's recording of the above was an exaggeration. However, *The Victoria County History* records *"... it is true that in 1866 there were at least nine well established public houses i.e. one for every 122 inhabitants of the parish."*

BENEFICIAL IN DROPSICAL COMPLAINTS...

Not all local drink led to *"mischiefs and irregularities"*: some were famed for their more sober and, indeed, medicinal properties - which may have even cured the effects of any "excesses". The following is taken from a national encyclopaedia.

"TILBURY - waters, in medicine, is an acidulous or saline water issuing from a spring, situated near a farm-house at West Tilbury, near, Tilbury Fort, in Essex. This water is of straw colour, soft and smooth to the taste, but leaving, after agitation in the mouth, a small degree of roughness on the tongue; it throws up a scum variegated with several colours... This water is esteemed for removing glandular obstructions, and hence is also recommended in scurvies and cutaneous diseases; it is good in bloody fluxes, purgings, and the like: in disorders of the stomach arising from acidity... and immoderate flux of the menses. As a diuretic, it is beneficial in dropsical complaints. It gently warms the stomach, strengthens the appetite, and promotes digestion. The usual dose is a quart a day."

E. Chambers, 1783.
Cyclopaedia or an Universal Dictionary of The Arts and Sciences...

TO A GREAT EXTREMITY...

There were many people who were willing to testify to the most remarkable curative properties of Tilbury Water, for a whole range of conditions.

"I Henry Davy in Finch Lane, ware-houseman, had the piles to a great Extremity in the middle of last June that my life was in danger... I sent to Mr Kelaway in Broad-Street for Six Bottles of the Alterative Tilbury Water; Before I had taken all, I found the pain of the Piles mitigated, and the bleeding entirely ceased. I sent for six Bottles more, and continued taking them, and now am in perfect health. I do testify this to be the Truth, this 24th day of July 1736."

Henry Davy, 1736.
In J. Andree, An Account of The Tilbury Water, 1779.

RIDING PROUDLY ON THE TIDE...

Returning to Thurrock's link with the Thames, it is difficult to ignore *"... one of the finest institutions in England"* - the various Training Ships, moored off Thurrock's shore, whose purpose it was to train young citizens for a life at sea.

"Reader, have you ever been to Grays, the station next to historical Purfleet, on the London and Tilbury line to Southend? If not, let me tell you that it is not a large place, nor a nice place either. Still, this struggling township on the Thames is worth visiting. Almost within the shadow of its tiny red brick house lies one of the finest institutions in England for the making of sailors, and soldiers, and citizens - for the making of men.

Proceeding a short distance along the main street towards the river the traveller will be brought face to face with this civilizing centre. He will see a huge, bold, sturdy vessel riding proudly upon the ebbing and flowing tide, moored about a hundred yards off the shore. This splendid three-decker, of 3,106 tons displacement and with a measurement of 220ft by 59ft, is London's training ship Exmouth.

The vessel's ninety-one portholes still proclaim its original character - that of a man-of-war... Its complement of 600 lads, its Captain Superintendent, and staff of officers still more eloquently testify to its intimate connections with the defences of the country - with the Navy and the Army, with the development of patriotism and citizenship. For, from this training ship have gone forth about 5,700 youths, well equipped for the struggle of existence, and not less well trained to battle with winds and waves and the treachery of oceans deep..."

Dr. Ch. H. Leibbrand, 1899.
The Strand Magazine Vol. XVII

AND OTHER STIMULANTS...

The *"Exmouth"* was not the first training vessel to be moored off Grays. Prior to the *"Exmouth"*, the training Ship *"Goliath"* had a tragic end when it burnt down to the waterline and sank a few days before the Christmas of 1875. The following is a contemporary account written by the then Head School Master.

> *"The inhabitants of Grays acted most kindly on this sad occasion, many women took off their petticoats to cover the naked boys, and other flocked down to the water-side, with any garments they could collect together in a hurry. As may be imagined, our boys presented a rather motley appearance.*
>
> *In spite of their shock and confusion they had experienced, in spite of the exhaustion they had suffered, the young seaman still remembered what they had been taught on board.*
>
> *Those who were injured in any way were at once put to bed... Many of the villagers in their eagerness to restore the failing energies of the rescued ones, brought brandy and other stimulants; of which the sufferers refused to partake, so strong an impression having been left upon their minds, by a lecture delivered on board the "Goliath" by a clergyman of the Church of England Temperance Society, a few weeks previously."*
>
> *R. J. Fenn, 1876.*
> *The Burning of the Goliath.*

By 1st February 1876, 16 bodies had been washed ashore. Among those who perished was Richard Wheeler, Assistant Schoolmaster to Mr Fenn.

A BEQUEST TO ENGLAND...

For the young seaman and their charges the day of the disaster was one of great courage. The tragedy was widely reported in the national press. The nation's heart was so touched by the event that, almost immediately, a nation-wide appeal was started to assist those in need. The following letter was received, offering a contribution to the fund.

London, January 11th

My Dear Lord Mayor,

Though much burdened with other claims, I cannot help taking advantage of the kindness with which you have inaugurated help for the "Goliath", and requesting you to accept, though but a poor mite, the utmost I can afford - £10 - for the purpose, believing, as I do, that these training-ships leave a much better legacy to the country in these depauperised subjects, and well-trained sailor boys than if, as Lord Shaftesbury said, we left a legacy of £100,00 though I wish I had it to leave for such a purpose. Every so trained, and depauperised boy, is a bequest to England worth making. With best wishes and three cheers for the success of all such Training-ships, I beg that you will believe me, my Lord Mayor (with many apologies, because I am ill).

Ever your faithful servant.

Florence Nightingale.

Florence Nightingale, 1867.
(In) The Burning of the Goliath.

WITH THE SPEED OF THE WIND...

Thankfully the training ships were not always involved in such calamitous drama. There were more mundane diversions that broke the daily routine on board, but nevertheless made news-worthy reports.

"The Evening News of March 2nd [1898], under the heading 'Seal Hunt in the Thames', gives the following narrative: Much excitement was caused at Grays, a correspondent reports, by the appearance of a seal on the mud flats opposite the training ship, 'Exmouth', seemingly making frantic efforts to reach the water. Several boats from the ship put off to try to capture the creature, which seemed tired out. The men expected no trouble in their undertaking but as the boat approached it, the seal dashed with the speed of the wind into the water, and after giving the boats a little chase, finally dived and disappeared, to the great disappointment of the ship's boys, who were eagerly watching the chase."

The Essex Naturalist. 1897-1898.

WHATEVER OF INTEREST IS TO BE SEEN...

Other, larger, marine mammals are occasional visitors to the shores of Thurrock, and always cause much local interest. As recently as 1996 a minke whale was washed up at Purfleet: although at 15ft and 1½ tonnes, it was a small specimen, compared to the visitor of 1887.

"Early on Wednesday morning a whale was found cast on the river's bank a little above the entrance to Tilbury Docks, its head reaching nearly to the top of the sea wall. Some coastguardsman were sent to watch it, and in the afternoon it was towed to the East and West India Dock Company's derrick, and lifted on to three trucks and taken to the engineers' yard.

A large number of persons from Gravesend and elsewhere went to see it previous to its removal, and the occasion was improved for the benefit of Gravesend Hospital, by placing collecting boxes very prominently before the visitors. After its removal to the yard, the Public were allowed to in inspect it m payment of 6d; the proceeds to go to the hospital funds, the Dock Company throughout showed their usual readiness to permit visitors to see whatever of interest is to be seen in the Docks, and the happy thought of benefiting the hospital will no doubt be appreciated by the Governors.

A large number of persons examined the animal on Thursday and it was stated that it would remain on view till sold, It is claimed by the Crown, and Mr Emmett, receiver of wrecks, was in charge, assisted by some of the coastguards. The whale measured 35½ feet in length and its largest girth was at first estimated as 13½ feet, but then accurately measure, was found to be 18½ feet.

The mouth measured six feet across, and its tail eight feet. Its weight was 6½ tons. Its skin is black and quite smooth, having the appearance of a well fitted kid glove. It has a huge mouth, and from the upper jaw hang the curious appendages known as whalebones: black and hard without, but lined within with white fibrous substance. The tongue is red, and with the bottom of the mouth is composed chiefly of blubber, soft and yielding to the slightest touch. On the top of the head is the blowhole, in form something like the head of and arrow. In the skin are a number of old scars, round, as if from the effects of bullets...

As to the reason for coming up the river, there are always plenty on eels and shrimps in the Docks, but on Tuesday a shoal of sprats appeared and penetrated the Main Dock, so numerous that they could easily be taken out without any utensil. It has been thought that while the whale came up the river in pursuit, but of course it is impossible to express any definite opinion on this point."

Grays and Tilbury Gazette, Oct. 1887.

LIKE OTHER STRANGE WAIFS...

An earlier whale off Grays, met a similar fate. The appearance of this whale seemed to provoke more local disputes regarding ownership, as well as more in the way of private enterprise.

"In the afternoon of Tuesday week, several labourers in the employ of Messers. Meeson, lime-merchants, at Grays, had their attention drawn to a dark object floating in the Thames, which appeared to be a vessel keel upwards. Its violent plunging, however, soon caused the observers to change their opinion. The tide was low, and they forthwith perceived it to be a whale, hard and fast ashore on the Black Shelf, a shoal abreast of Grays. Boats were put off, and with much difficulty the whale was secured with ropes, when it proved to be a "finner", measuring fifty-eight feet in length, and thirty in girth. As the tide flowed, arrangements were made to haul it on shore; and as the water floated it, desperate were the attempts made by the creature to regain its freedom. The ropes, however, held it fast; it was dragged to land, and there killed with a sword. The labourers were of Triculo's opinion that the monster would make a man and not a holiday fool but would give a piece of silver to see it: a screen was soon raised about the carcase [carcass], and the captors were soon in the way of making a handsome sum by the exhibition of the prize.

This Whale, like other strange waifs, is likely to be the cause of litigation. On Saturday, the Lord Major, attended by the City solicitor, proceeded to Grays, for the purpose of officially asserting his claim to the creature, as Conservator of the River, and giving it up to the service of the captors, upon condition that they would not convey it to London or Gravesend for exhibition, not allow it to become a nuisance anywhere. His Lordship, upon the spot where the Whale lay,

*experienced the desirableness of insisting upon the latter
condition; for the stench had already become very great. No
sooner was his Lordship's intention of given up the prise
announced, than there sprang up a number of claimants, at
the head of whom was Captain Corbet, who, with his men,
first pursued the whale, and, by aid of some watermen,
secured it. The Lords of the Admiralty made no claim to it as
a droit, having received experience from a precedent in 1809,
when they were put to great expense in defending their claim
to a whale taken in the river, but which was demanded by Sir
Charles Flower, then Lord Major, and entitles to all the
"Royal fish" caught within the City Limits; and to his
Lordship the whale was ultimately adjudged.*

*There is no small animosity among the captors, the sum of
£150 having been offered for the carcase [carcass], which is
rich in oil; but they have been recommended to refer their
claims to the arbitration of Captain Ronaldson, the principel
harbourmaster. Meanwhile, the exhibition at Grays is
flourishing at Trinculo's price - 6d. a head."*

The Illustrated London News, 1849.

TO HER EXTREME CONTENTMENT...

Retaining this maritime theme, and that of visitors arriving along the Thames, any anthology of Thurrock's past cannot pass without reference visit of Queen Elizabeth I to Tilbury in 1588. It was at Tilbury where the mass of troops were assembled, ready to defend not only Thurrock but also the nation, against the arrival of the Armada.

"On the 8th of August Elizabeth arrived in her barge at Tilbury Fort... and was welcomed by a royal salute from the Block-house, with a grand display of banners, and the exhilarating sound of martial music. Escorted by a thousand horse, she proceeded to the camp, per carriage, being, as we are informed, 'overloaded with diamonds, emeralds, and rubies.' Having slept at the house of Mr Rich, early next morning she witnessed a sham battle, performed by the troops, to her extreme contentment. Previous to quitting the camp, she gave to the sergeant-major, a gracious message to be delivered to her soldiers which... has been called her speech at Tilbury."

Elizabeth Jane Brabazon, 1864.
A Month at Gravesend Containing an Account of the Town & Neighbourhood.

MY HONOUR AND MY BLOOD...

Elizabeth's 'Tilbury speech' was delivered to the assembled troops: a speech ranking as one of the most inspiring of all time. On Thurrock's shores the following words were spoken; on Thurrock's shores the defence of the whole of England was thought to rest.

"... Let tyrants fear... I have come amongst you, as you see, at this time, not for my recreation and disport, but being resolved in the midst and heat of battle, to live or die amongst you, to lay down for my God, and my kingdom, and for my people, my honour and my blood even in the dust.

I know I have the body but of a weak and feeble woman; but I have the heart and stomach of a king, and a king of England too; and think foul scorn that Parma or Spain, or any prince of Europe should dare to invade the borders of my realm; to which rather than any dishonour shall grow by me, I myself will take up arms, I myself will be your general, judge, and rewarder of every one of your virtues in the field.

...we shall shortly have a famous victory over those enemies of my God, of my kingdom and my people."

Queen Elizabeth I.
West Tilbury, 8th August 1588.

Thanks to the detective work undertaken by Randal Bingley, former curator of Thurrock Museum, we now know where, in West Tilbury, these words were uttered. As Colin Elliot remarks in his book *'Discovering Armada Britain'* this area *"... should be one of the most hallowed pieces of English ground..."*, although at present, and with some lament, he reminds us, *"... not so much as a plaque marks the spot".*

EVOKE THE GREAT SPIRIT...

I n drawing this collection of writings to a close let us, through the eyes of Conrad, return to again to the Thames. The following piece seems to summarise the essence of this local anthology: looking back on the people and on this landscape, both served by that great river - *"By Thames to all peoples of the world"*.

"The old river in its broad reach rested unruffled at the decline of the day, after ages of good service done to the race that peopled its banks, spread out in the tranquil dignity of a waterway leading to the uppermost ends of the earth... Indeed nothing is easier... than to evoke the great spirit of the past upon the lower reaches of the Thames... The tidal current runs to and fro in its unceasing service, crowded with memories of men and ships it had borne to the rest of home or to the battles of the sea... What greatness had not floated on the ebb of that river into the mystery of an unknown earth!... The dreams of men, the seed of commonwealths, the germs of empires."

Joseph Conrad, 1902.
Heart of Darkness.

HE WORKED STRANGE ACRES...

Writings from the past, produce evocative images: images of then, of now; of contrasts, of similarities. To add a more comtemporary perspective; in remembering the past, we should also not forget to see the present. Interesting, evocative, even strange sights can still be observed. On the death of a local farmer, at Stanford-le-Hope, the following was written:

> *"(He) worked strange acres, an ancient landscape bordered by those science-fantasy backdrops of Shellhaven. No darkness ever fell over his enclosures, all was illuminated by the spasmodic flame of blazing gases in the sky... He did not worship the past - too shrewd a farmer for that, but he respected the land, its origin, its men and implements. He saw the debt he owed to machinery now obsolete."*
>
> *Randal Bingley, 1974.*
> *Panorama, The Journal of the Local History Society.*

Let us too *"... not worship the past",* but simply respect the land, its origin, and its people, whilst not forgetting to take more than a passing glance to see and protect what is still with us.

In conclusion, we turn to the words of Richard Pusey (1987), who reminds us of the need for continuity, for roots, and of the importance *"... not only to conserve what we can of our visual heritage but to treasure even the echoes of our past. Not to have this wider perspective on the years is to condemn ourselves to a loss of empathy with those who have made their pilgrimage before us."*

SOURCES

Allen, D.H. *Essex Quarter Sessions Order Book, 1652-1661*. Essex Record Office Publications. Chelmsford: Essex County Council. 1974.

Andree, J. *An Account of The Tilbury Water...* (4th Edition) London: John Ellison, 1779.

Bannister, T. *The Recollections of a Septuagenarian. In The Journal of the Thurrock Local History Society*. Number 2. 1957.

Belloc, H. *The Historic Thames*. London: J.M. Dent & Sons Ltd. 1914.

Berkeley, G. *Life and Recollections*. Vol. IV. 1866. Cited in *Belhus and the Barrett-Lennard Family* compiled by I.G. Sparkes. 1964.

Bingley, R. *Panorama, The Journal of the Thurrock Local History Society*. Number 18. 1974.

Black & White Magazine. *A Strange and Novel Deep Thinkers' Home at Stanford-le-Hope. Black & White*. Sept. 1910.

Bodle, R.E. *H.M.S. Resolution at Purfleet. Panorama, The Journal of the Thurrock Local History Society*. Number 23. 1980.

Brabazon, E.J., *A Month at Gravesend containing an Account of the Town & Neighbourhood*. London: Simpkin, Marshall & Co. 1864.

Brayley, E.W., Britton, J. *Beauties of England and Wales: Essex. Vol. V.* London: Vernor and Hood. 1803.

Brown, A.F.J. *Quarter Sessions Order Book, 20 April 1762. English History From Essex Sources 1759-1900*. Chelmsford: The County Council of Essex. 1952.

Buchanan, R. *Andromeda: An Idyll of the Great River*. London: Chatto & Windus. 1901.

Chambers, E. *Cyclopaedia or an Universal Dictionary of The Arts and Sciences....* Vol. IV. 1783.

Chamber's Journal, 1864. In *Purfleet*. Sparks, I.G. 1963.

Clark, Percy. *Vanishing Essex Villages: an Undiscovered Corner*. In *The Essex Review*, Vol: XII, No: 43. 1902

Coller, D.W. *The Peoples' History of Essex, a Narrative of Public and Political Events...* Chelmsford: Meggy and Chalk. 1861.

Conrad, Jessie. *Joseph Conrad and his Circle*. London: Jarrolds Publishers, 1935.

Conrad, Joseph. *Heart Of Darkness*. 1902.

Conrad, Joseph. *The Mirror of the Sea*. 1906.

Defoe, Daniel. *A Tour Through the Whole Island of Great Britain*. 1725.

Dickens, Charles. *Great Expectations*. 1861.

Elliot, C. *Discovering Armada Britain*. Newton Abbot: David & Charles Publishers plc. 1987.

The Engineer. 21st October, 1864. In *Panorama. The Journal of the Thurrock Local History Society*. Number 28. 1986.

Essex Field Club Journal. Vol. IV. 1885-86.

Essex Field Club Journal. Journal of Proceedings at Ordinary, Field, and Other Events For February 1883 to January 1887. 1892.

The Essex Naturalist Vol. II. 1888.

The Essex Naturalist. Vol. IV. 1897-1898

Fenn, R.J. *The Burning Of the Goliath*. London: Shaw and Sons. 1876.

Gibbens, Wm. *The Essex Review*. 1902.

Goodsall, R.H. *The Widening Thames*. London: Constable. 1965.

Grays and Tilbury Gazette. Oct. 1887.

Grays and Tilbury Gazette. Nov. 1891.

Grieve, H.E.P. *The Rebellion and the County Town*. In (Eds.) Liddell, W.H. and Wood, R.G. *Essex and the Great Revolt of 1381*. Essex: Essex Record Office. 1982

Hayston, J.R. *The Thurrock Historical Society Journal*. Thurrock Local History Society. 1959.

Heygate, Rev. W.E. *Alice of Fobbing: or the Times of Jack Straw and Wat Tyler*. London: Henry and Parker. 1860.

Hissey, J. In Lindley, P. (ed) *New Holidays in Essex*. Undated c. 1890.

Hughson, D. *Circuit of London: Being an Accurate history and Description of the British Metropolis and its Neighbourhood....* Vol. 6. 1809.

The Illustrated London News. Vol. XV, No. 395. 20 October 1849.

Kentish Independent. 8th October, 1864.

Knighton, H. *Chronicon*. (Ed J.R. Lumby, 1889-95) in R.B. Dobson - *The Peasants' Revolt of 1381*. (2nd Edition). Macmillan Press. 1983.

Leibbrand, C. H. *The Strand Magazine*, Vol. XVII. 1899.

Lindley, P. (ed) *New Holidays in Essex*. undated c. 1892

Loftus, E. *The Tilburys* (1949) In (Ed) Sparkes, I.G., *Tilbury: Town and Docks*. 1964.

Moore Place. *Moore Place Social Settlement and Guest House - Guide to Visitors*. c.1911.

Munro, J. *Pioneers of Electricity...* 1890. In *Purfleet*, compiled by I.G. Sparkes. 1963.

Neal, W. *With Disastrous Consequences: London Disasters 1830-1917*. Enfield: Hisarlik Press. 1992.

Palin, Rev. W.J.T. *Stifford and its Neighbourhood: Past and Present*. 1871.

Palin, Rev. W.J.T. *More About Stifford and its Neighbourhood*. 1872.

Pennant, T. *A Journey from London to Dover.* 1784. In *The PLA Monthly* Vol IV. Port of London Authority. March 1929.

Pepys, S. *The Diary of Samual Pepys,* (Ed.) R. Latham and W. Mathews. London: Bell and Sons Ltd.

Petaval, J.W., *Vegetarian Messenger.* May, 1911.

Powell, W.R. (assisted by Board, B.A. and Knight, N.) *The Victoria History of the County of Essex.* Vol VIII. Oxford: Oxford University Press. 1983.

Pusey, Richard. *Essex: Rich and Strange.* London: Robert Hale. 1987.

Runciman, J. *Gravesend to the Nore, Chapter XII, The Thames, from Source to the Sea. (In) The Royal River.* Cassell and Empanly Ltd.

Sparkes, I.G. *Belhus and the Barrett-Lennard Family.* Upminster. 1964.

Sparkes, I.G. *Purfleet.* Upminster. 1963.

Stoker, B. *Dracula.* 1897.

Strutt, J. *Queenhoo Hall.* In Smith, C.F. (Ed.), *An Anthology of Essex, Collected by I. Lucy & B.M. Gould.* London: Sampson, Low, Marston & co. Ltd. 1911.

An Anthology of Essex. London: Sampson, Low, Marston & Co. Ltd. 1911.

Wallace, Alfred Russel. *My Life: A Record of Events and Opinions.* Vol. II. London: Chapman and Hall Ltd. 1905.

White, W. *Eastern England from the Thames to the Humber* Vol.II. London: Chapman & Hall. 1865.

White, W. *History, Gazetteer and Directory of the County of Essex - 2nd Edition.* 1863.

Young, A. *A Six Week's Tour Through the Southern Counties of England and Wales - 3rd edition.* Straton, Nicholl, Cadell, Collins & Balfour. 1772.